Location Writing

Taking Literacy into the Environment

CAROLINE DAVEY · BRIAN MOSES

David Fulton Publishers

To the children and staff of Amherst Junior School (C.D.)

And for Anthony Masters (1940–2003) who pioneered location writing with children and alerted me to its many possibilities (B.M.)

David Fulton Publishers Ltd
The Chiswick Centre, 414 Chiswick High Road, London W4 5TF

www.fultonpublishers.co.uk

David Fulton Publishers is a division of Granada Learning Limited, part of Granada plc.

The right of Caroline Davey and Brian Moses to be identified as the authors of this work has been asserted by them in accordance with the Copyright, Designs and Patents Act 1988.

First published 2003

10 9 8 7 6 5 4 3 2 1

British Library Cataloguing in Publication Data
A catalogue record for this book is available from the British Library.

ISBN 1-84312-045-3

Typeset by Kenneth Burnley, Wirral Cheshire
Printed and bound in Great Britain

Contents

Acknowledgements

Thanks are due to the following copyright holders for permission to reproduce poems.

'Frogspawn' by Brian Moses, from *I Wish I Could Dine With a Porcupine* (Hodder Wayland, 2000).

'Entering a Castle' and 'The Bonfire at Barton Point' from *Don't Look At Me In That Tone Of Voice* (Macmillan, 1998).

'If I Were A Shape', first published in *'The Works 2' – Poems on Every Subject and For Every Occasion*, Brian Moses and Pie Corbett (eds) (Macmillan, 2002).

'Letter From a Roman Soldier', first published in *Stories From the Past* (Scholastic Collections, 1994).

'Palm Tree Talk', © Lydia Fulleylove.

'The Flint', © Jean Kenward.

'Girl with a Worksheet in a Castle', © Fred Sedgwick.

'Beachcomber', © George Mackay Brown, reproduced by permission of John Murray (Publishers) Ltd.

Faber and Faber Ltd, for extracts from 'Cow III' by Ted Hughes, from *What is Truth?* and *Poetry in the Making*, also by Ted Hughes.

Note: throughout this book, OUP refers to the Oxford University Press.

We gratefully thank the following schools for allowing us to reprint material by their pupils:

Amherst Junior School, Guernsey
Fletching CP School, East Sussex
Freda Gardham CP School, Rye
Chesworth School, Horsham
Moira House School, Eastbourne
Marshlands CP School, Hailsham
Little Ridge CP School, St Leonards-on-Sea
Melrose Ladies College, Junior Department, Guernsey
South Harting School, Petersfield
Cleves Junior School, Weybridge
Sark School

Kent College, Junior Department, Pembury
St Michael's School, Withyham
Nutley CEP School
Village Schools' Association, East Sussex.

We also thank the children from Able Writers' Weekends at Northcourt Manor, Isle of Wight.

If anyone else feels that they should be credited please contact the publishers and amendments will be made in subsequent editions.

Introduction

Location writing is an attempt to encourage a more imaginative and creative response to the environment than that which is generated by worksheet-based activities. Wherever you choose to write on location you should explain to the children that you want them to sketch their impressions in words and make a record of how the place makes them feel. By using the details that they observe, the children's writing will reflect a feeling of realism and truth and will bring fresh insights to prose and poetry that are not always possible to obtain in the classroom.

A view from a hill once promoted the following observations:

- Two cars play tag where a road splits the fields.
- Cows hold a powwow.
- The line of pylons are motionless martians, standing on parade.

Another young writer looked at a tree that had been struck by lightning and saw:

a tall, thin finger pointing to heaven.

In his book *What is the Truth?*, the poet Ted Hughes best exemplifies this sharpness of observation when he writes:

And there's a ruined holy city
In a herd of lying down, cud-chewing cows.

Absolutely, that's spot on, as of course one would expect from a master craftsman, but I had never looked at cows in that way before and his freshness of vision is exhilarating.

Hughes also offers advice to young writers regarding how to write imaginatively about a subject:

Just look at it, touch it, smell it, listen to it, turn yourself into it. When you do this, the words look after themselves, like magic.

In this way, Hughes says, the subject will be captured.

Writers, of course, are ideas detectives. They keep notebooks and record anything of interest – something someone says, a slogan from an advertisement, a strange street name and so on. They train themselves to be observers, to use their senses.

Children need to be observers too and an effective way to really get them thinking about small important details is to try the following exercise.

Tell them to imagine that they will be moving house at the weekend and to think of what their house would look like once it was stripped of its furniture. Ask them to make a list of the things they would miss about their houses.

Most children will write about missing their bedrooms, but what makes a bedroom special? Everyone has a room in which they sleep but what makes one child's room different from another? Not the furniture, that will be gone. Maybe it's a mark on the wall, or a creaking floorboard, or strange noises from the radiator. This is the challenge for children. What makes their room special?

Children should be asked to investigate this for homework, to become ideas detectives around their homes. What makes other areas of the house special too? What else will they miss? What about the garden, what's different about that?

If I left my house I'd miss star gazing on top of the flat shed roof
and the family of wriggling grass snakes under a large flat stone.
I'd miss the dense clump of trees right at the back of our garden
and the loud shrill buzzer Mum would press when it was time to go for supper.

Eleni Bohacek

Outside of the classroom children need time to write effectively. Time to look and listen, to wander, to look again from different angles, and to read any relevant information. It is a totally different approach from the completion of a fact-collecting worksheet in a certain amount of time before moving off to another venue.

Initially, try to steer children away from rhyme if they are writing poetry and encourage them to say what they really want to say. A repeating phrase or line is often a good technique to use as it helps to give the poem a rhythm. Make sure also that children know that spelling and neatness are not important at the drafting stage. They can be tackled later when the finished piece is edited.

If you offer children an idea to get them started, do let them know that this is only a launch pad. The best writing will take the original idea and stretch it, resulting in different slants. A fresh way of looking at something should always be encouraged.

Writing in an imaginative way is not in the least like maths. There are no right answers to be obtained. Writing is about thinking of something to say, and then afterwards thinking again, finding a more interesting way to convey a meaning. Children often worry about getting it wrong and need constant reassurance that what they write first of all is often just a stepping stone to another idea that's an improvement on the first.

The right approach is vital and the attitude of the teacher is all important in developing children's writing. This needs to be done in ways that will both challenge children and channel their ideas. Once their first ideas have been written down, children should be encouraged to build upon them. Do this by praising, questioning, offering fresh challenges and showing obvious excitement about what is being written.

Girl with a Worksheet in a Castle

There's a castle we visit where Mr Barret talks
battlements, baileys and barbicans.

But when I've done my worksheet and my sketches,
down unsafe stairs I find this lonely place,

this earth-floored larder. I breathe deeply in
the stink of centuries. An ancient chef

sweats. Humps sacks of onions, spuds,
turnips and garlic. Thinks of wine and oil

he'll baste over mutton, pork or fish. I hear
salt Saxon shouts. Alone, I'm history

and history is me. But still . . . be still . . .
Then
Mr Barret's calling *Eleanor Smith!*

He asks me about battlements and baileys,
and, not this lonely place, this worksheet.

Fred Sedgwick

Preparation for visits

Many of these points will be obvious but they will serve as a quick checklist and you will probably wish to add others!

1. If possible visit the location before you take the children, in order to find out exactly what is there. You will need to know where toilet facilities are, if your trip is going to take the whole day, where you and the children can have a packed lunch and what the arrangements will be if the weather is bad.
2. You may need to prepare work for the day and/or set trails which the children will follow on the visit.
3. You may need to fill in forms for health and safety and organise off-site visit consent from parents.
4. The websites relevant to your particular location need to be checked before the visit, or at least before the children use them for research.

5. Make sure you have enough adult help on the trip; the more help, the smaller the groups can be.

6. Ensure you take a first aid kit, mobile phone with relevant numbers noted and spare pencils and paper. Someone always loses their pencil over a high wall or in the water!

7. Make sure the children remember clipboards and paper or their jotters.

8. Take the school camera, digital, still or movie. You may need to use images when you return to school.

9. Ensure the children are dressed appropriately for a particular visit. If they are going to be doing a lot of walking, high heels are not a sensible option!

10. Obviously prepare the children beforehand. Explain where they will be going and what they will be expected to do on the trip. They might like to do a little research of their own at home, before the visit.

11. Arrange the children in groups before you leave school. Give the helpers a list of children in their group and insist that they constantly check that they still have the right number of children!

How to use this book

This book is for teachers at KS2. It provides a range of ideas for location writing, alongside examples of the kind of work that children write in response to the various subject areas. It contains 19 lesson plans linked to objectives in the literacy framework, which may be followed at various locations. It also includes further ideas, background material and photocopiable resource pages. Most of the ideas should be flexible enough to be scaled up or down according to the age group.

The book can be consulted prior to any school visit and appropriate ideas selected for use. These can then be prepared so that children receive guidance on location. Alternatively, teachers can teach from the book itself using examples given as a stimulus for children's own observations and written work. On some occasions it will be sufficient to follow just one theme. At other times children can follow a range of ideas that will eventually link together to form part of a trail. Advice on how to set up a trail may be found in Section 1.

The School Environment: A Writers' Trail

The school environs are an obvious place for location writing and if there are school grounds it makes sense to develop them as a learning resource. A writers' trail can be set up and ideally this should have eight or ten stopping points where children can be stimulated to write in a variety of genres. Each point on the trail should then have a range of activities to suit children of different ages and abilities. Some of the ideas for writing will come from the children themselves: initially a small group of older children can act as trail coordinators, making suggestions as to where the stopping points should be located and the kind of writing that might be pursued there.

Points on the trail can be given interesting names to aid identification, names which may promote ideas for writing themselves. For example:

1. Lily Pad Pond
2. Treetop Hill
3. Crusoe's Cabin (gardener's hut)
4. Dragon Ash (site of bonfire)
5. Bramble Bench (a meeting place)
6. Ivy Archway
7. The Dark Den (back copse shelter)
8. The Hurricane Tree
9. The Gateway to Adventure
10. The 'Y' Tree (tree shaped like the letter Y)
11. The Burial Mound (raised area of grass in shape of oval)
12. The Quiet Area

(From the trail at Chesworth Junior School, Horsham)

Consider first how your trail will be routed. Are there obvious starting and finishing points? The following are ideas of locations for points along a trail.

1.1 THE SCHOOL BUILDING

Perhaps the school building itself might be a starting point.

Amherst School, Guernsey

Lesson One

The Making of our School.

Learning Objective

To identify the different purposes of instructional texts, for example, recipes and the use of imperative verbs.

Resources

Recipe books, examples of poems, jotters, the school building.

Task

Discuss the words used when explaining the method for a recipe. For example, mix, stir, blend, and beat. Make a list on the board. Take the children outside to look at the school building and tell them they are going to write a poem about their school, setting it out like a recipe. Children make notes in their jotters about the materials used, the shapes they see and objects in the playground.

Using the recipe words, together with their notes, invite the children to suggest some lines for a poem. Write them on the board, emphasising that the first words need to be verbs, such as beat, blend, mix and so on.

Let the children work on their own or in pairs to write their own poem.

Differentiated Task

Lower ability groups could draw part of the school building or playground and add words and short sentences around the picture.

Stir in a stone wall

Blend in some rocks

Beat well   SCHOOL

Add a spoon of sand

This is my school

Extension Activities

This format can be used on any building or at any location.

Cross-curricular Links

ICT – poems can be typed and a digital image of the school inserted.

A Place for a Story

Talk about the importance of place in stories. Can children think of books that they have read which have a very strong sense of place? Are there any interesting parts of the school that might be included on the trail as stimulus for story writing?

Many ideas for stories occur when someone asks the question, 'What if . . . ?'

What if a snowman came alive?
What if you could walk through a door at the back of a wardrobe and discover a fantastic land?

Are there any 'What ifs' that might start stories connected with the school building? The following are examples of places that might be used as trail points, particularly if the school is an older building.

The School Bell

In an old school building there may be a school bell. What if the school bell rang at midnight?

Alternatively write a list poem:

When the school bell rang at midnight . . .
The sky cracked open and light slipped through.
The shadows hugged each other.
The silence dissolved into peals of laughter . . .

For an idea of setting out this poem and a poem on a similar theme see 'In the 13th Hour' (*Catapults & Kingfishers* by Pie Corbett and Brian Moses, OUP, p. 97).

The Cellar

Perhaps there is a cellar. Describe the cellar steps and doorway. Write down five words or phrases that show what it looks like or how it makes children feel.

Talk about urban myths and the ways in which these can spread. Are there any school myths connected with the cellar? If not, start one up!

Is there a locked door? A locked door serves two purposes: it is locked to prevent anyone getting in; it is locked to stop something getting out!

Would anyone dare to enter the cellar at night?

In *Gowie Corby Plays Chicken* by Gene Kemp (Puffin), Gowie is dared to spend the night in a ruined cellar under his school.

The Boiler House

Describe the boiler house. Again, write down words and phrases that show us what it looks like or how it makes children feel.

Ideas for a story could include the boiler house ghost, someone imprisoned there, aliens planning their invasion of Earth from the school boiler house, the nasty headteacher's lair . . .

A Turret/Attic Rooms

Who lives in the turret? Invite children's suggestions. Maybe the occupant is an old sea captain staring out of the window and remembering the days when he was captain of a ship. Maybe an ancient headteacher or a wizard. What would the turret room look like?

What would the occupant of the room see as he stared down from his turret, on the tops of trees, at the people and traffic below? What would he be thinking about? Who would he be remembering?

Read the Gregory Harrison poem, 'Alone in the Grange'. Children might use this poem as a model for their own writing. Discuss how the writer builds up an atmosphere. Why does he use repetition of single words? Who is he?

Entrances and Exits

Gateways and doorways are powerful images in literature. Can children think of stories where the action moves from one world to another? – Harry Potter via Platform 9 $^3/_4$; The Philip Pullman trilogy – *His Dark Materials: Northern Lights, The Subtle Knife, The Amber Spyglass*; *Tom's Midnight Garden* by Philipa Pearce; *Elidor* by Alan Garner; the *Narnia* books by C. S. Lewis, are all good examples.

Discuss the magical implications of a gateway. Where might it lead? How do you pass through the gateway from one world to the next? Can you feel it happening? What do you need to take to keep you safe? Are there guardians of the gateway?

Possible gateways might be goalposts at midnight with the moon shining down and indicating a pathway between the posts, or the space between two trees.

Alone in the Grange

Strange,
Strange,
Is the little old man
Who lives in the Grange.
Old,
Old;
And they say that he keeps
A box full of gold.
Bowed,
Bowed,
Is his thin little back
That once was so proud.
Soft,
Soft,
Are his steps as he climbs
The stairs to the loft.
Black,
Black,
Is the old shuttered house.
Does he sleep on a sack?
They say he does magic,
That he can cast spells,
That he prowls round the garden
Listening for bells:
That he watches for strangers,
Hates every soul,
And peers with his dark eye
Through the keyhole.
I wonder, I wonder,
As I lie in my bed,
Whether he sleeps with his hat on his head?
Is he really magician
with altar of stone
Or a lonely old gentleman
Left on his own.

Gregory Harrison

Example of Recipe Poem

The Making of Our School

Take two tons of bricks
Mix with cement and sand.
Stir well until blended thoroughly.
Add glass to the window frames
Squeeze cleanser and
Rub in until smooth and shiny.
Next gather together some children and teachers.
Blend them together into the learning pot.
This makes my school.

1.2 THE PLAYGROUND

List games currently being played on the playground. What are the rules for these games? Can they be written down so that everyone agrees with them?

What games have been played on the playground in the years since the school was opened? Make a list of games and crazes. Contact former pupils of the school if possible.

Playground skipping games

List things that are said on the playground and string these together to compose a chant-like poem in a similar vein to Alan Ahlberg's 'I Heard It In the Playground'. The poem should have a chorus and could feature a range of voices and instruments.

Contrast the noise and bustle of the playground by day with the silence of the playground at night.

In the midnight playground
a sleepy owl I see.
In the daylight playground,
a pigeon perched in a tree.

Has the playground got a voice and if so what would it say? Would it moan or complain?

How would children feel if they found themselves standing in the deserted playground at midnight? Children could invent a playground ghost and write a report about it. Who has seen the ghost? Where has the ghost been seen? When was the ghost alive? Who was it? A short story *The Shadow Cage* by Philippa Pearce (Puffin) might be worth reading here to help set the atmosphere.

The Playground Snake

Another 'What if . . .' opportunity. Many schools have number snakes in the infant playground. What if the playground snake slithered into the school?

To start with, take children on a walk through the school building and allow them to note down as many words beginning with 'S' as they can find.

Next, talk about verbs beginning with 'S' that might suit the movement of a snake – slither, slip, slide, spiral, spin, scare, etc.

Now write a poem that begins . . .

If the snake in the playground slithered into school it would . . .

Forget rhyme, but a rhythm can be established by beginning each line with 'It would . . .'

> If the snake in the playground came into school
> it would slither through the corridor,
> it would slide into the staff room,
> It would spiral on the sick bed.
>
> It would slip into the sink
> and swirl round the taps.
> It would scare the children.
> It would show the face of danger.
>
> Francesca Folmi, Year 3

The play-
ground
snake

What if a snake slithered into school?

It would be sick in the school sink,

It would snuggle to sleep in a shoe box.

It would scramble around someone's scrummy tummy.

It would spit poison as it slides over the teachers,

It would swallow slippery soap from the shower,

It would pay no attention to the No Smoking sign,

It would slither to the secretary and scare her half to death,

AND FINALLY it would smile at Mr Steer as it strangled him!

Year 3

Further ideas for similar alliterative poems might focus on different creatures – 'When the cat crept into our classroom', 'When the fly flew through our fire exit', 'When the rabbit ran into the room'.

These could be turned into picture books where children can practise writing for a different audience, i.e. younger children in the school. Before starting however, children should research picture books to discover how the best ones are set out. It is important to consider carefully how the writing and pictures are placed on the page. A variety of approaches will be far more interesting than simply a series of pictures with the writing underneath. Point out too that pictures should be bold and colourful as well as acting as visual texts in their own right. A total page count of 8, 12, 16 or 24 pages should suffice. Children could work in pairs taking it in turns to write and illustrate.

1.3 A SCHOOL POND

A school pond might feature in a writers' trail.

Lesson Two

The Amazing Pond Creature.

Learning Objective

To write poetry that uses alliteration and similes to create effects.

Resources

Poem by Daisy, 9 years (see page 12).

Task

Take the children out to the pond and list any creatures that are spotted in and around it. Add any other creatures that the children suspect may be living in the pond.

Choose one of the creatures listed, give it a name and a character – Freda the Frog, Tess the Tadpole, Wallace the Water-snail, Duncan the Dragonfly.

Describe the creature, make it larger than life. Think about its size, shape, appearance, strength, speed, colour, noise, food, drink and special features.

The children can work in pairs, drafting a poem which includes alliteration and similes. For example:

Freda the Frog,
Is as green as emeralds.

Their finished poems can be performed to each other.

Extension Activities

Finish a story that begins 'A tragedy happened to Thomas Toad on his way to the pond . . .' (or any other creature). Brainstorm suggestions.
Examine frog-spawn – make detailed notes of what it reminds you of.

Frogspawn

All those commas
waiting to be born
out of frogspawn.

All those wrigglers
waiting to wriggle.

All those dots
about to hop.

Watch them quiver,
slide and slither.

A city afloat
or musical notes

that wriggle away
from the bars of a song,

'We won't be long'
they sing.

Brian Moses

Cross-curricular Links

Art – the imaginary creature can be drawn as a cartoon character. A story board can be created in comic strip style, recounting the creature's adventures at the pond. This will help with sequencing if they then write a story.
Science – can be linked to the Year 4 QCA unit Habitats.
ICT – type up finished and corrected version, adding suitable clip art.

Examples of Written Work

Frilly Frog is as big as the world
She's as strong as my dad
Stronger even than Hercules.
She's green with red spots
And likes wearing stripy dresses.
She's as fast as a motorbike
And makes a noise like our head teacher
When she's teaching us.
She can jump into the sky
And likes to sleep in my bed
She's really cool at basketball.

Daisy, aged 9

Freda the emerald green frog
Catches flies with her long elastic tongue
As fast as a thunderbolt.

Eli

Fizzy the fish is very fast and zips through the water like a roller coaster. She's red and blue and looks like electricity when she swims.

Madeline

1.4 WALLS AND HEDGEROWS

Ask children to think of reasons why walls and hedgerows are important places for small creatures. They offer shelter for plants to grow and thrive, and protection for small creatures to live and breed. Here children might hunt for mini beasts. How many can be identified along the length of a wall? Can children see any mini beasts living in and around a hedge? Make up a dictionary of mini beasts for this location.

Children might find it rewarding to conduct a month-by-month survey of a hedge to discover the sort of plants and creatures that enjoy its protection. Their findings might be set out as below.

Position of hedge:

Date:

Time:

Plants noted:

Creatures spotted:

The growth of particular plants could be measured and sketched.

A holly hedge is a good protection for many creatures. Ask children to examine a holly leaf. Brainstorm words – spiky, prickly, shiny, the leaves are spiteful. Try to look at the leaf in different ways. What creature does it make you think of – perhaps spiky, spiny creatures such as porcupines, hedgehogs and mythical creatures such as dragons. Use these observations to compose haikus (3 line poems, 17 syllables, 5 in the first line, 7 in the second, 5 in the third).

Write a diary for one of the mini beasts encountered – a day in the life of a spider, slug, wood louse, etc. (Prior to any writing it would be useful to discuss how events are recorded in diary form.)

The Diary of Millie the Millipede

Wednesday 15th July ... Ouch! My 139th leg on my left side got crushed last night, it hurts more than ever now. I hope it gets better soon. Mum says we can go to the Millival tonight for a special treat. But I won't be able to go with a bad leg, will I?

Thursday 16th July ... We did go to the millival last night, it was really good. We went on all the rides. Mum was nearly sick on Spiders' Revenge. But I have to go to the doctor-pede about my leg.

Holly

Children could also write stories – What happens when an insect grows in size? An ANT turns into a GIANT! What made it grow and what happens? Write a newspaper headline and story to cover such a bizarre event.

Write also from the point of view of a creature that's misunderstood. A snail was inspiration for the following piece.

> If you were a snail you would understand that
> we are great and proud,
> we are rulers of the slow world.
> There is no point in being fast, it is a let down.
> If you were a snail you would understand that
> slow is cool, slow is useful.
> You really should be green with envy
> when you know what slow can mean.
> If you were a snail you would understand that
> being slow is great.
> So we'll show you (slowly).
>
> Emma Leech

Children could write similar pieces – from an ant, earwig, caterpillar or whatever is encountered on the trail.

Make mini beast picture books based on creatures seen on the trail. Look at Eric Carle's books *The Very Hungry Caterpillar*, *The Bad Tempered Ladybird*, etc. Take a woodlouse on an adventure. Perhaps an ant travels from one point on the trail to another. Who and what does it encounter along the way?

Wonderful reads which will give children a totally different view of insects are two books by Paul Shipton, *Bug Muldoon and the Garden of Fear* and *Bug Muldoon and the Killer in the Rain*. These are stories about a private investigator in the insect world . . . 'the best sleuth in the whole garden. But right now I'm having a bad day. My legs are aching – all six of them.' Great inspiration for children's own stories.

1.5 TREES

Trees will probably feature at some point along the trail.

The old
oak tree
stretches
out its
arms

Lesson Three

This Old Tree.

Lesson Objectives

Writing poems using active verbs and personification (making the tree appear human). Using repetitive words to create rhythm.

Tasks

(A). Find a suitable tree or trees in the playground or school field. Talk about the tree appearing to be human, i.e. personify the tree. Let the children suggest some phrases, such as:

> The tree stretches out its arms,
> Leaves dance in the wind.

Make a list of six or so phrases that could be used later in a poem.

(B). Ask the children to think about the sort of questions they have always wanted to ask a tree. They might like to work in pairs, one asking the questions and the other responding with the answers. For example:

Tree, why have you got needles so sharp?
I have needles so sharp to prick the wind.

(C). Use a repeating phrase to begin a poem. This will help to strengthen the poem and make it sound good when it is read aloud. If trees could talk they would be able to tell us about all the things they have seen and heard since they were first planted. Children could begin with:

This tree . . .

What might the tree have seen and heard? Let the children suggest ideas, for example, the changing seasons, buildings demolished, laughter, arguments, cheers of crowds at the school sports, traffic and birds.

(A)

The tree stretches out its arms, catching the leaves, dancing in the wind.

Branches wave rhythmically in the gentle breeze that brushes against them.

(B)

Tree, why have you got needles so sharp?
I have needles so sharp
To prick the wind, when it tries to blow me down.

Tree, why are your bony fingers so long?
I have fingers so long so that I can hold all the birds safely in their nests.

Tree, why are you so tall?
I am tall so that I can look down and survey all the world's joys and wonders.

Tree, why are you so old?
I am old because I am the bearer of all wisdom and the guardian of the ground.

Tree, tree what have you heard?
I have heard the laughter of children, the destruction of buildings, and the cry of pain.
I have heard the animals talking and the arguments of couples.

Rachel

(C)

The Old Tree

This tree hears the ding dong
of bells when there is
a wedding.

It can see silver stars
come out at night.

This tree provides a tower
for the evil rooks to guard.

It lets the ivy creep all around it.
This tree sometimes has children
climbing on it.

It has branches for them to hold.

This tree has seen birds being
hatched out of their eggs.

It has had branches chopped off
and you can see where it has
healed.

Thomas Phinn

1.6 BIRDS

Let children listen to the sounds around them. Can they hear evidence of birds in the area? Are any birds visible? Are the birds in groups? If so, how do they look? Brainstorm some words – seagulls strut, pigeons waddle, sparrows hop, crows look like black cowled monks or gangsters. Overweight pigeons are fat-bellied cargo planes. Encourage children to extend their observations into short prose pieces or poems.

Collect poems about birds for a bird anthology.

Do birds wake up in the morning, as we do, with shopping lists in front of their eyes, with the day planned out ahead, or is everything done by chance?

Children will enjoy composing shopping lists for birds – what do they want to buy and where will they do their shopping? Allow imagination free rein here. *Birds do their shopping at Worms R Us!*

Kestrel's Shopping List

Spider flan
hop-pot
vole juice
claw file
beak sharpener
mouse soup
wholemole bread
weasel sausages
worm spaghetti,
vole-au-vent
etc.

Mark

Birdsway Supermarket

Mother blackbird went to the
supermarket and bought:
Twelve juicy worms,
seven huge black beetles,
a handful of hairy spiders,
a bunch of fresh green grass,
nine squashy slimy maggots,
eight shiny, giant bluebottles,
a large, wet, muddy leaf,
seventeen cherry flavoured slugs,
a few creepy crawly ants
and a carton of extra thick
snails' cream at half price.

Class 3 Shared Writing

Consider also where birds go at night, where they go on holiday and what they dream of:

A bird dreams of jumping to the moon
in one big bounce.
It dreams of living in a big house
instead of a small nest.
A bird dreams of swimming, swimming
in the sea
And of knowing how to do everything
like a very smart something.

Kathryn

Children will enjoy composing bird raps —

What goes into a magpie's pie?
A juicy fat worm and a big frog's eye,
a bit of bacon found in a bin,
chips from McDonalds, cut very thin, etc.

1.7 FLOWERS

The following activity will be most useful in summer when butterflies are about.

An Iranian poet once wrote of butterflies as 'Love letters exchanged by flowers'.

Look at some of the flowers in this area and think of others around the school grounds. Children might like to think about what various flowers might say to each other. What might a dandelion say to a rose, a violet to a bluebell or a daisy to a sunflower? What messages might flowers send to schoolchildren? Do daisies want to be picked and made into daisy chains?

What messages might flowers send?

Lesson Four

Message to a Sunflower.

Learning Objectives

To write from another character's point of view. Ask questions and impart information from their point of view.

Resources

A flower bed in the school grounds, or park. Examples of messages.

Tasks

Look at the variety of flowers in the school grounds. Think about the sorts of things the flowers might say or ask each other, especially a smaller flower to a larger flower. Discuss the children's ideas. Encourage them to jot these down, in their rough books. Work in mixed ability pairs to produce a message. Imagine what a taller flower, a sunflower, might see that a dandelion could not.

Read out a selection of finished messages, discuss each other's.

Extension Activity

Suggest they might like to work on a response to their message. (See examples.)

Cross-curricular Links

Drama – act out your message and response.
Science – identify the different parts of various flowers. Draw from observation and label.
Art – produce large colourful paintings/pastel drawings of flowers.
ICT – type up poem and insert an image or add clip art.

Examples of Messages

Dear Sunflower,

Tell me what you see?
I can only guess.
You are tall; the breeze must bend your stalk,
The rain must injure your yellow petals.
Do bees linger awhile on your head?
My view is of ants hurrying about their business.
And worms dodging the bird's eager beaks.
Please tell me what you see?

From Dandelion.

A response might be:

Dear Dandelion,

My view is of children happily playing
And yes the strong breeze does bend my long stalk
But I'm strong and can bounce back.
Rain bruises my yellow petals, sometimes.
Bees do gather in groups on my head
The noise can be deafening.
I see birds on high branches.
When the next breeze blows, I'll look for you below.

From Sunflower.

1.8 ROUND AND ABOUT

At any point along the trail children can use their senses and make observations:

Dark clouds . . . like shadows in the night.
Trees waving in the wind . . . like monsters with spiky hands.
Hammering . . . like an angry woodpecker

They can carry out scavenger hunts to find objects – a stone, a 'skeleton' leaf, bark from a tree, an interesting piece of wood. With older children talk about simile and metaphor at this point and then ask them to use these devices when looking at their own objects. What does the object look like? What does it remind you of? Does it look like something else? What does it feel like?

It's possible to start with a chart:

Real (objective)	Unreal (subjective)
autumn leaf	like a hand
veins	like fingers
fragile	skeletal
etc.	etc.

Some children might like to turn their objects into cartoon characters and involve them in stories or comic strip adventures. This could be a chance for paired writing.

Reassure children again that there is no wrong way of looking at something and that ideas may be as fanciful as they wish.

Riddles could also be written referring to different points on the trail. A view might be described or noises heard at that point. Other children then have to guess the place that is being written about.

Imagine what happened at a particular trail point – last night, last week, last year. Write a newspaper report of the event. Interview any witnesses and include a photograph of the location.

Conclude
the trail in
a quiet
area

Finishing the trail

A quiet area of the grounds would be a good place to conclude the trail so that children can gather and share the work that they have been doing.

Classes could then produce a data bank of resources to back up the trail. This would include picture books, fiction, poetry, information books, websites, equipment, etc. The data bank should indicate where the resources are to be found and if they apply to any particular stopping point on the trail. Anthologies could be put together on various themes – trees, birds, playgrounds, etc. These would include both prose and poetry written by children working on the trail and also that by professional writers. Classes should also suggest further resources that could be acquired.

Once the trail is complete, it can be put on to the computer so that classes or groups can obtain a printout of the ideas that stem from whatever point they are concentrating on. A mini guide to the school grounds could also be produced. This could feature the trail, and parents could be invited in to walk the trail, try out some of the activities and hear some of the work that the trail inspired.

2 Castles, Houses and Ancient Monuments

Castles have immense potential for stretching children's imaginations.

Prior to any visit children need to be introduced to the chosen castle by way of photographs, maps, word lists, local legends and guidebooks.

Pose various questions for the children to consider both before and during the visit. For example:

- How would you capture this castle?
- How would you escape from the castle?
- Where would be the best place to set a story?
- If you were the castle ghost which part of the castle would you haunt?
- If you were locked in the castle at night, what would you do?

2.1 ENTERING A CASTLE

On the visit itself begin at the castle entrance by considering how a castle should be entered.

How should a castle be entered?

Lesson Five

How to Enter a Castle.

Learning Objective

To write in a definite pattern and to use similes, metaphors and interesting adjectives that describe ways of moving.

Resources

A castle, or ancient historic building, the poem by Brian Moses, 'Entering a Castle', examples of poems etc. written by children, jotters.

Task

On arrival at your chosen castle, stop and look at the entrance to it. Ask questions, for example:

How should a castle be entered?
Should we go quietly,
should we enter with a shout,
should we crawl or charge?

Ask the children to write down some different ways of moving, e.g. march, crawl, walk, barge.

Think about similes or metaphors you could add, e.g. enter quietly like a speechless child, or, noisily like a roaring bear, or push and shove like a rushing wave. Back in the classroom these ideas can be used to create a poem with a definite pattern.

Children on Guernsey describing Castle Cornet wrote these examples in a definite pattern:

You can creep like an ant
Or stamp like an elephant.
You can march like a soldier
Or tiptoe like a spy.
You can push and shove like a piece of the sea.
Or you can be brave and climb the walls.

Laura

You can enter a castle crestfallen, like a cheerless ant.
You can enter it quietly, like a speechless mum.
You can enter noisily like a roaring bear.
You can enter a castle as if you were a wonderful magician ...

Nicola

Differentiated Task

The children could draw the entrance to the castle and add the movement words around.

Digital photographs could be printed for the same activity.

Extension Activities

All castles and buildings have an entrance, so this activity can be transferred to any location if a castle is not easily accessible.

Cross-curricular Links

ICT – the digital camera can be used to take different photographs of the entrance at different angles. These can then be used in the differentiated task.

Science – linked to QCA Unit 3C, Characteristics of Materials. The building materials of the castle can be explored and properties discussed.

Entering a Castle

Don't enter a castle quietly
or timidly,
Don't enter it anxiously,
ready to bolt
at the slightest sound.
Don't enter it stealthily
taking slow and thoughtful steps,
considering with each footfall
the mystery of history.
Don't be meek
or frightened to speak.
For when you enter a castle
you should ***charge*** through the gate
and signal your arrival with a **SHOUT!**
You should play the invading army
and ***barge*** a way through.
You should ***swagger*** up to the door
then **shove** it aside and announce,
'Here I am! This is mine!'

This castle is here, it is waiting for you,
and today,
it is yours for the taking!

Brian Moses

2.2 OMENS

How spooky is the place that you are visiting? Walk children around the grounds of a castle or historic house and ask them to look for omens. These can be quite ordinary things which when grouped together could well be warnings of spooky activity.

Omens

I heard the cuckoo with no food in my stomach,
I heard the stock-dove on the top of the tree,
I heard the sweet singer in the copse beyond,
And I heard the screech of the owl of the night.

I saw the lamb with his back to me,
I saw the snail on the bare flag-stone,
I saw the foal with his rump to me,
I saw the snipe while sitting bent,
And I foresaw that the year would not
Go well with me.

Traditional, Gaelic

I saw a flower rotting on the ground,
I saw a stream with still water,
I saw a young tree being strangled by ivy,
I saw a dial without sun.

I heard rain on leaves,
I heard a horse neigh with fear,
I heard the crows cawing.

They were omens of things to come
and that thought made me shiver.

Liam Harrison

The bell sung lazily, echoing around the garden. I turn.
A bird swam around the tower once, twice, three times.
The rain eyed me up greedily, then spat. I run.
Out of the corner of my eye I saw trampled flowers.
The horses screamed. Around me all bad omens hurled.

Emma Clover

(Both of the above examples were written during a spooky weekend for young writers at Northcourt Manor, Shorwell, Isle of Wight.)

2.3 CASTLE GHOST

Children may enjoy researching their castle to try to discover whether there are any reported ghostly sightings. They could interview members of the staff who work at the castle.

   As they tour the building, ask children to imagine what the castle ghost might look like, where it might dwell, and the places it wanders through. Collect words and phrases from observation of the castle so that when the figure is created, it will be obvious that it belongs to the castle.

Dunstan-burgh Castle

> I found the ghost of the castle
> Between the prison walls,
> his body was old and crooked,
> His bones were brittle and cold.
>
>   Chloe

Consider what clothes it wears, how it moves, what it does:

   Marching stiffly with a face of granite.
   Wearing his faded uniform
   of black, gold and red.
   Hearing the waves crash against the wall,
   Fighting a battle against the wind.

Think of the ghost's hopes and fears, this may help with the ending to the poem:

His cold lonely face
Begs for company
For fear he would be alone for eternity.

When the poems are written ask children to swap with each other and then try to draw their partner's castle ghost from the details that are written down.

(Further ideas and examples of poems about 'spirits' or 'phantom figures' may be found in 'The Seashore' section, Lesson Plan 3.2 'The Sea Spirit', page 59.)

2.4 PAST AND PRESENT

The wonderful thing about historic buildings is the interplay between the past and the present. The present is all around us but so are the clues that allow us to imagine what these places were like in past centuries.

Lesson Six

What the Castle Heard/Saw . . .

Learning Objective

To write poetry that features similes and metaphors, and uses sound to create effects, for example, onomatopoeia, alliteration, distinctive rhythms.

Resources

A castle, examples of poems, jotters.

Task

A castle holds many clues that allow us to imagine what it was like centuries ago. Ask the children to think about what the castle may have heard in the past. Suggest some ideas, such as cannons firing, soldiers marching up and down, or the cries of prisoners. As the children walk around get them to write down their ideas. Include sounds and alliteration. For example:

the crashing, booming thunder of cannon fire,
swirling, circling swallows.

The children's words and phrases can be used in a poem that has a definite pattern. Begin like this:

The castle sees . . .
The castle hears . . .

Repeat every other line or just explore a single sense:

The castle sees . . .
The sea, a blue sheet with lacy white edges,
The boats, rocking like babies in a cradle.

The castle sees . . .
The greedy sea gobbling up the rocks
As it gallops urgently to St Peter Port.

The castle sees . . .
Houses having a chat to their neighbours,
Piled up on top of each other like chairs in an Olympic Stadium.

The castle sees,
Town getting dressed for the summer!
Rainbow umbrellas swirling like dancers on the stage,
Bright flowers, blobs of paint on an Impressionist's palette,
Excited flags whizzing and looping like kites,
And tiny people sprinkled like happy hundreds and thousands.

The castle sees . . .
Guernsey, with a smile as big as a hug.

Group poem, Year 3

What does the castle see?

Differentiated Task

Children can use their ideas about what the castle hears, sees or feels in a poetry template. They can be given the initial words of each line on a worksheet:

The castle once heard . . .
The castle now hears . . .
The castle once saw . . .
The castle now sees . . .
The castle once felt . . .
The castle now feels . . .

Extension Activities

Combine what the castle heard with what the castle saw and felt centuries ago. Another idea is to write about all the things that the castle sees, feels and hears today, thus writing in the present tense.

The past and present can be combined in the same poem and children should compile two lists while exploring the castle. One list can be headed 'Now' and the other 'Then', for example cannons/mobile phones.

> The castle once heard the thunder of the firing cannons,
> But now hears the sound of the bleeping foghorn.
> The castle once saw great warships coming from the sea,
> But now sees sailing boats and ferries.
>
> Jenny

Other comparisons can be made between the castle by day and at night, between the different moods of the castle in summer, winter, spring or autumn, between good weather and bad.

Cross-curricular links

History – could be linked to QCA Unit on Tudors, or the Second World War, depending on the castle used.
ICT – set up a database of who has used the castle and why.

Differentiated Resources

A further connection between past and present might be made via artefacts. The castle museum will probably house archaeological exhibits that were found in the castle environs. Children could be asked to choose an exhibit – pottery, weapons, clothing, toys, stones – and to think about that exhibit's connection to the past. They might think about the people who lived there before the castle was built. The following poem by Jean Kenward could provide useful guidance. Note how each verse begins with a question.

The Flint

Who lived in these ancient woods?
Many thousand years ago
small men made their dwellings here –
lugged the great stones to and fro
and beneath a sheltering bough
ate, and slept, as I do now.

Who last held this flint? I guess
someone sharpened it to be
a precious weapon . . . kept it safe . . .
used it often, skilfully, carved an arrowhead, and slit
the creature's throat he slew with it.

Who felt spirits in the trees?
Saw the sun rise like a god
on its journey east to west?
Who sniffed water, understood
where it wandered through the ground
and marked the spot it might be found?

Who walked on this ancient track?
Short and muscular, he wore
skins to cover him, and lit
fires to warm the winter's core.
In my hand (how strange it is!)
I hold the flint he held in his.

Jean Kenward

2.5 IF THE WALLS COULD TALK

It is often said of historic buildings that we would know everything about them if their walls could talk. If you visit somewhere that involves a guided tour, suggest that the guide steers clear of too many names and dates, concentrating instead on stories and anecdotes that will help to bring a building to life.

At Hammerwood House in Sussex, visitors are always impressed by the exploits of children who once lived in the house and particularly how they used to climb out of their nursery window on to the roof. From here they would make their way to the kitchen roof and drop pebbles through the skylight into bowls of food below. Extra points were scored if these dishes actually reached the dining room and were discovered by the diners! Detail like this will help to make children's writing sparkle.

Prior to writing ask the children for alternative words for 'talk' – gossip, complain, grumble, shout, laugh, joke, cry, confess, whisper, tell about, etc.

If these walls could talk
they would complain
of the children running up and down the hall.
They would gossip
about the maid who works in the kitchen.
They would joke
about the new born baby.
They would grumble
about the harp and its loud music.
They would laugh
about the stones in the porridge.
They would confess
that everything in the house they love
(except for the harp.)

(Group poem)

Sam's walls have had enough:

We keep on having to have nails plunged into us
with paintings hanging onto us, it's like torture.
We keep on having to wear different wallpaper
every time somebody else moves in.

2.6 EMPATHISING WITH HISTORICAL FIGURES

Focus on particular historical events that happened at the historic building. Find out about them from guidebooks, exhibitions and Internet sites.

Try to empathise with historical figures and consider what they must have felt like. Did the castle house prisoners? Sit down in a particularly gloomy part of the building and imagine . . .

Did prisoners walk here?

Prisoner's Walk

A dark, gloomy passage only used to exercise prisoners. The only sound would be the gulls screeching above, the sea below crashing on the rocks. Only the sky to stare at. No way out, only a wall to climb, if only you had the strength. Guards on the look out all the time. Occasionally the cannons would fire and someone would let out a scream.
A hateful place. Miserable prisoners, petrified and scared about being hurt and having to die in the castle. No chance of escape.

Mark

Tell children that somewhere in the castle there is something that was buried many years ago. They then need to find a suitable place where this event might have happened and consider the following questions:

- What was buried?
- Who found it?
- Whose was it?
- What happened?

Children may interpret these questions as widely as they wish but once they have answers they should try to weave their ideas into a story. Do the events that took place in the past have repercussions in the modern world?

2.7 LETTERS HOME

Children could write letters from those who may have been held in the castle against their wishes or from soldiers who were stationed there. It is important to talk through ideas here and to foster a serious atmosphere for writing so that the children can really begin to empathise with what people from the past may have felt.

Lesson Seven

Letter Home.

Learning Objective

To write a letter linked to work in other subjects, for example, history.

Resources

A castle or other ancient monument, examples of letters.

Task

Castle Cornet, in Guernsey, has many clues to its past inhabitants. Guernsey was occupied by German forces during the Second World War and many of the German troops were stationed at the castle. Their gun emplacements can still be seen and some soldiers carved above the entrances the names of their wives and girlfriends they had left behind.

The German soldiers were probably homesick and certainly wouldn't have wanted to be where they were, particularly during the rough storms of winter and in the later years of the war when food and supplies were scarce.

The children could imagine they are one of the soldiers stationed at the castle. Ask them to write a letter home to their family. Talk through ideas first, encouraging the children to empathise with what the soldiers may have felt.

Read the examples to show the children the kinds of things they could write about.

Letter Home

My Darling Urzal,

I am writing to feel warm with your love. It is very dull here and the wind is whipping my face as I write this. In the summer the weather here is lovely and we sunbathe on sentry duty and play cards when we're off duty. In winter it is a different story. Storms sweep in across the sea and Guernsey seems to attract them!

(from a German soldier – 1942)

Dear Sister,

Now it is winter on the island. Storms have been sweeping us.
The food is just dry bread and water and the sergeant makes us watch him while he dines on pâté and red wine. I wish I could come home, the hours are too long. Yesterday I worked from 6 in the morning until 11 at night. I have been spared a little time to write to you. The supplies of chocolate you sent me were confiscated. How is mother? Is her bronchitis better? Please send some chocolate and biscuits.

Yours hungry, tired and deprived.

Hans

(from a soldier stationed in Castle Cornet during the Second World War)

Differentiated Task

Children could write down words and phrases which might describe how they, as a soldier, may be feeling, so far away from home. These adjectives and phrases could be written around an outline of a German soldier.

Cross-curricular Links

History – QCA Unit 9, What was it like for children in the Second World War? Unit 18, What was it like to live here in the past?
ICT – children could use the Internet to find out all they can about the occupation of the Channel Islands. Two useful websites are The Occupation Society, www. occupied.guernsey.net and Island Life, www.islandlife.org. Both sites contain links to other very useful sites.

Extension Activities

All castles and ancient monuments hold clues to the past. This activity can be adapted and used in other locations, as long as historical events that happened at the chosen location are well researched.

Examples would be letters from Mary Queen of Scots at Fotheringhay Castle just prior to her execution, or from Anne of Cleves, exiled to Richmond Palace because Henry VIII found her unattractive. Letters could also be written from the point of view of Roman soldiers stationed on Hadrian's Wall.

Letter from a Roman Soldier

Although Roman legionaries were not supposed to marry, many had 'unofficial' wives and children. The following is a copy of a secret letter dictated to a paid scribe by a Roman legionary, Tiberius, stationed on Hadrian's Wall, and addressed to his 'family' in Camulodunum (Colchester).

My darling Flavia, we have been parted for too long now. I grow bitter at the delays and false news that greets my every enquiry as to when I can expect a transfer south. I know that I am voicing the feelings of many when I say that I hate this posting. If it isn't the ceaseless rain or the sleet that penetrates even my thickest tunic, it is the boredom of sentry duty that drives me to despair. Occasionally we see action when rebellious northern tribes fling themselves at the wall, but more often than not our days are filled with patrols and fatigues. Of these, cleaning the toilets is by far the worst duty. Maximus, our officer, he doesn't get his hands dirty, he just barks out the orders. Three times a month we have to strap on full kit – armour, weapons, cooking pots, camp building equipment – and march for 20 miles. If our feet are blistered or attacked by frostbite, this can be agony.

There's something about the landscape here that hardens the heart. It is rugged scrub land across which the wind blows relentlessly, even in summer. I still feel the cold even on days when the sun is strong. I still suffer with lice too and no matter how hard I try to rid my tunic of these creatures, they always return. There are some pleasant times of course when my companions and I are in good humour. We joke and tell stories, visit the bathhouse and indulge in gambling.

Sometimes I ask myself, why did I join the Roman army? I know that the pay is good, I'm fed and clothed, and I wanted adventure, but stationed here at the very edge of the Roman Empire, in this cold, wet and misty land, I don't think that this was quite the adventure I had in mind. One day, when I complete my 25 years' service, we will be married and I will take you to Rome. I shall buy some land with my pension and our sons will farm the soil and have no need to follow their father's footsteps.

Until that day, my dearest Flavia, I must content myself with thoughts of you, our children and home.

Tiberius

(The poem 'Roman Wall Blues' by W. H. Auden is worth tracking down and reading in association with the above as it gives a vivid picture of the harsh conditions at the Wall.)

Alternatively write a rap that puts across a similar message:

The soldiers on the Roman Wall
really had no fun at all.
All they ever did was moan,
they knew they'd rather be at home.

(Chorus)
Hey, ho, here we go,
another day of rain and snow.

2.8 IDENTIFYING SHAPES

For a cross-curricular activity, try linking poetry with maths.

Lesson Eight

If I Were a Shape . . .

Learning Objective

To write a list poem using adjectives and similes. To invent calligrams and a range of shape poems, selecting appropriate words and careful presentation.

Resources

Castle or ancient monument, jotters, examples of poems, e.g. 'If I Were a Shape' by Brian Moses.

Task

Any location can be used for this piece of creative writing. While the children look around a castle or ancient monument, ask them to note down as many different shapes as they can and to indicate where they spotted them. Back in the classroom, the children can work on developing a list poem, beginning with the phrases:

> 'If I were a shape at . . .
> I'd be a square picture frame
> surrounding a famous General . . .'

> If I were a shape at Michelham Priory
> I'd be an irregular flagstone walked upon by a
> thousand monks,
> I'd be an arch, wide and proud, holding up
> more than my own weight.
> I'd be a sphere, a sour but juicy crab-apple ready
> to fall from a tree.

(Michelham Priory is near Eastbourne in East Sussex)

Differentiated Task

The children could pair up to work on their list poems. They could write one line describing each shape, then illustrate their work or use a photograph.

Extension Activities

The children could concentrate on shapes, for example, an archway. They can then write down six words or phrases that describe the look, the colour, or how the shape makes them feel. For example:

Arch shaped, like a halo,
Surrounding the door,
Grey-blue granite stones
towering above the entrance
making me feel like a dwarf

The poems could be written as calligrams or shape poems, if practicable.

An
archway –
with teeth?

Cross-curricular Links

Maths – link this to maths work on 2D and 3D shapes.
ICT – take photographs of some of the shapes. These can be used to illustrate the poems.

If I Were a Shape

If I were a shape
I'd be a rectangle,
I'd be a snooker table with Mark Williams potting the black,
I'd be a football pitch where Spurs would always be winning,
I'd be a chocolate bar that you could never finish,
If I were a rectangle.

If I were a circle,
I'd be a hoop rolling down a mountainside,
I'd be a wheel on a fast Ferrari,
I'd be a porthole in Captain Nemo's submarine,
If I were a circle.

If I were a cone,
I'd be a black hat on a wicked witch's head,
I'd be a warning to motorists, one of thousands,
I'd be a tooth in a T Rex's jaw,
If I were a cone.

But, If I were a star . . .
I'd be Robbie Williams!

Brian Moses

2.9 COUNTDOWNS

Younger children may prefer to use their observational findings in a countdown poem. This time get them searching for numbers. Find something around the castle or house to link with numbers from 1 to 10.

Turn the traditional form around and count up if you prefer:

One shiny golden coloured clock,
Two multi-coloured flags waving in the wind,
Three black empty archways,
Four dangerous musket steps ready for battle.

and so on up to ten, or further if required . . .

and thousands of stones all holding up this castle.

Younger children may also enjoy considering who actually lives in the castle now. List the creatures that might inhabit the modern-day building – spider, mouse, rat, woodlouse, duck, pigeon, seagull, bat, carp; or perhaps some people from the past – prisoner, jester, lord, magician, ghost.

Write as a countdown poem or suggest that children write from the point of view of one of these creatures or people . . .

I am the spider who lives in this castle,
I see . . .
I listen to . . .
I remember . . .
I dream . . .

2.10 PROPERTY FOR SALE

Prior to visiting a castle or historic house, collect together various estate agent's sheets giving details of houses for sale. Let the children examine these and work out the way in which the details are set out. They could practise writing an estate agent's sheet for their own houses.

While on the visit tell children that they will be required to 'sell' the castle or historic house and that they should look at it through the eyes of an estate agent. Obviously it won't be possible to include everything, rather they should try to spot the best selling features and include these in their descriptions of the property. Remember that estate agents always look for selling points such as 'solid construction', 'south facing', 'extensive well-trimmed lawns', 'parking for several cars' and so on.

Remind children to sketch the building and include this on the publicity sheet. Can they attempt to put some sort of value on the property?

Lesson Nine

Hadrian's Wall for Sale.

Learning Objective

To write in an appropriate style and form to suit a specific purpose and audience. For example, a 'House for Sale' poster, exaggerating description.

Resources

Castle or ancient historic building. Examples of estate agent's descriptions of houses for sale, jotters.

Task

While visiting the castle or historic building, imagine how an estate agent might describe the place. Think where you might be able to exaggerate the look and structure (especially if it is in ruins), the content, surrounding outbuildings and amenities, and so on. Make notes as you walk around. For example, you might try to sell part of Hadrian's Wall:

When in Rome . . .

Have you ever fancied living in a wall? Not just any old wall but Hadrian's Wall?
Well, now is your chance. This huge stone monument is for sale.
Named after the great Roman General, Hadrian, there are fantastic views over the rolling countryside. Some rebuilding may be necessary, however there are plenty of spare stones lying around, which could be used! . . .

The phrase below was actually used in an estate agent's blurb:

> This property is a butterfly, in all her
> splendour, having emerged from an ugly
> brown chrysalis . . .

Use the description you have written to produce a poster with either a sketch or photograph of the house, or ancient structure for sale.

Differentiated Task

Children could work in mixed ability pairs, one concentrating on the illustration and the other writing the description.

Cross-curricular Links

ICT – search the Internet for estate agent sites that advertise stately homes or chateaux in France. Websites to use could be French Connection or Papillon Properties. Use the digital camera to take images of the building you are visiting. Use appropriate computer software to design the poster or booklet.

History – could be linked to the QCA Unit on The Romans.

2.11 MYTHS AND LEGENDS

If you are looking at myths and legends, don't immediately reach for the Greek myths or for Norse mythology; there are plenty of myths and legends to be found in our castles and ancient monuments which can provide a stimulus for written work and drama. Read a legend, or better still retell a legend, in the place where it originated. The legend will be better understood if children can picture the place that inspired it. Dunstanburgh Castle in Northumberland has its own legend involving caves and sleeping warriors.

It was the wildest of nights. Lightning split the sky and heavy rain had already drenched the lone figure on horseback as he journeyed along the Northumbrian coast. It was clear to Sir Guy that he needed to shelter until the worst of the storm passed by. The next lightning flash revealed the ruins of a huge building still some way off but Sir Guy urged his horse forward.

As he drew nearer he realised that what lay ahead were the twin towers and outer wall of Dunstanburgh Castle. Sir Guy rode through the archway in the castle gatehouse. Here, at least, he could shelter from the rain.

All at once, a shining apparition stood before the knight, beckoning him to follow if he wished to find 'the lady of his dreams'.

Sir Guy was taken through a labyrinth beneath the castle to a huge door which was opened by ghostly hands. The massive cavern in which Sir Guy found himself was lit by hundreds of candles. In their flickering glow he could make out a whole army of armoured warriors and their warhorses, still as statues, held by some kind of spell.

The shining figure led Sir Guy to the far end of the cavern where a crystal tomb was guarded by two skeletons. Within the tomb lay a beautiful lady, her cheeks wet with tears. One of the tomb's guardians held a horn, the other a sword. Sir Guy was then told that he had to choose either the horn or the sword. What happened to the lady within would depend on the choice he made.

Sir Guy stood thinking about what he should do for a long time and then made his decision. He snatched up the horn, blew loudly, and heard the notes echoing round the cavern. At that moment the horses snorted and began to stand, the warriors leapt up and unsheathed their swords. Sir Guy was transfixed by the lady in the tomb but as he gazed, her outline grew blurred and the whole scene faded. He felt as if he were falling down a long tunnel and as he fell he heard these words in his head:

Woe to the coward who blew on a horn when
he might have drawn a sword.

When Sir Guy woke the next day, he searched in vain for the entrance to the underground chamber and the lady whose spell remained unbroken.

There are many different stories about caves with sleeping warriors. Another Northumbrian castle, Sewingshields, is reputedly (along with many other locations) the site of King Arthur's Hall.

Exploring a castle or ancient monument can give pointers that will assist in any retelling of its legend. Children should be thinking about sound effects and visual stimuli that might be included in any class presentation. It can also be useful to design a storyboard for the legend while on location and to present it as a comic strip.

Further Work

This could involve writing a modern version of the legend. The Dunstanburgh legend might be set in a supermarket where you have to make a choice between one product and another. What happens if you make the wrong decision? Do you eat baked beans and nothing else for the rest of your days?

Compile a neighbourhood guide containing as many legends as you can find. In Whitby, for example, there is the legend of the Barguest, a demon that appears in the guise of a huge black dog. The awful roar of the creature is heard only by those who are about to die.

Investigate chivalry. Identify examples of chivalric practice – Sir Gawain pledges to marry an ugly hag if she will save his king's life and is honour bound to proceed with the wedding; Arthur's courage as he journeys to Mont-St Michel to slay the foul giant that is ravaging the country; Robin Hood capturing the Bishop of Hereford and distributing his gold pieces to those he has wronged in the past.

2.12 BAD WEATHER VISIT

If the weather isn't all that you had hoped for, use it to your advantage. Notice how the wind or the rain affect the place that you are visiting. Ask children to make notes and use these as the basis for their writing. These ideas come from first-hand observation:

> The curtains opened, the wind swifted in.
> It was alive, it was whispering and calling.
> It was breathing, nobody could understand
> what it was saying.
> It roared like a lion shifting its mane.
>
> Rain made the paths slushy like stones in a stew.
> It made thousands of concentric circles on the
> glistening lake.
>
> It hung like glass balls from the tips of big leaves

The Same Wind
(Castle Cornet, Guernsey)

> Even the seabirds have trouble riding
> the roller coaster wind,
> the same wind that rips its fingernails
> down walls
> till the castle is caught in its grip.
> The same wind that tunnels its way
> into passageways, squeals through arrow slits
> and is desperate to grab the scrap of flag
> and run away with it.
> The same wind that wakes up sleepy boats
> and flings them about to its violent beat.
> The same wind that blew through history,
> rattling the bars of prisoners' cages,
> puffing fresh life into what remained
> of the one who hung from the hanging place.
> The same wind that struggled to knock
> the castle off its rock.
> The same wind, blowing then, blowing now,
> blowing us.

Brian Moses

3 | The Seashore

The sights, sounds and smells of the seashore offer children a great variety of stimuli for location writing. There is a multitude of locations, from sand flats to towering cliffs, from busy harbours to quiet coves, from fishing ports to seaside amusements, and whatever the chosen location, begin by making observations.

3.1 THE BEACH

The following are observations made at a pebbly beach below cliffs:

- Foaming waves crashing against the shore, the glistening sea on the calm horizon . . . cliffs broken down by rough waves of many generations.
- Pebbles drawn by the force of the water.
- Pathway of foam.
- Cliffs like giants going to pounce.
- Clouds moving away at a leisurely pace.
- Path of shining water.
- Seagulls guarding the beach.

The children's observations can then be used as the basis for a poem about this particular point.

Cliffs tower above crashing waves

The Beach

Waves crash down on the shore sending foamy splashes
into the atmosphere.
Pebbles scatter and rattle as the bright clear ocean
smashes over them.
The force of the roaring waves push and pull the stones
closer, closer.
Closer into the secret depths of the beautiful living sea
Where schools of fish rule the reefs and guard
the hidden sea beds.
Back up above, the seagulls hover and glide

through the air,
Keeping a watchful eye over the seaside.
The cliffs tower above like giant hands waiting to grab
but are frozen in place.
Fishy odours fill the air and mix with the salty sea smell.
I wander between the sharp rocks,
The sun glistens, the ocean glitters.

Stacey Cummins

With many of these observations, Stacey is tuning into the sort of details that would not have come to mind so readily in the classroom, details that make her writing sparkle. Had Stacey not seen the pebbles scatter and heard them rattle as the waves smashed over them, it is doubtful whether she would have described them in this way. In the last two lines, Stacey's original intention was to write: 'I wander between the sharp rocks/the sun glistens making the ocean glitter'. In the final version she dropped the word 'making' and substituted a comma. This really does give a more satisfying and complete final line.

Hanora's observations are from the shoreline at Dungeness in Kent:

No seagulls, no noisy speedboats,
no rickety pier to walk along,
only a line of children
laughing and stumbling
along the borderline
between sea and sand.

Sabrina took a close look at Creux harbour in Sark:

The buildings, dented and marked and rusty
. . . crane stand,
a memory of when men launched boats by hand
. . . the bobbers, some sparkling new, some of old age.
A rusty old boat trailer, paint marks on it,
its life is nearly over.
Old bits of wood, marks all over,
oil stains as well, disgusting.

Sabrina might then look further at her notes and develop one particular line of thought. 'When men launched boats by hand' might well be the starting point for a poem about Sark in earlier times. She could also consider the 'rusty old boat trailer'

– what type of life did it have, who used it, what type of boats did it carry? There may well be scope to talk about personification here (thinking of an object as if it were a person). 'The boat trailer sleeps all day in the sun, its joints are old and stiff, it can't move as fast as it used to.'

Scavenger hunts

A stretch of beach can turn up all kinds of interesting finds. Send children out on a scavenger hunt. Ask them to find three things: (a) an interesting stone, (b) a shell, (c) something thrown away. (Gloves would be good for this activity.)

Remind children about similes and metaphors before they begin any writing about what they have discovered. Choose one of the objects and begin by asking questions:

- What does the object remind you of?
- What does it feel like?
- Does it look like something else?

This is also the moment to reassure children that there is no wrong way of looking at something and that ideas should not be dismissed as being too fanciful.

The Three Stones

The first old stone is worn
like it had been in a war
and lost some limbs.

    The second old stone
    has got eyes of wisdom
    as if it has seen everything.

        The third old stone is scratched,
        like cave men have carved on it
        words of long ago.

My stones hold knowledge,
so please tell me your secrets.

Laura Martin

Driftwood

Our driftwood is
a duck's neck as it flies to the river.
It's a rabbit burrow, deep underground,
The horn of a charging bull at a bullfight,
It is a dolphin diving and leaping.

Our driftwood is
A Saxon drinking horn full of mead.
A quill pen copying the words of the Bible,
It is a dagger with gold and jewels.

Our driftwood is whatever we want it to be.

Group writing

Everyone is familiar with the idea that the sound of the sea can be heard within a shell, and although most shells on British beaches will be too small to hear very much, the idea may well promote some interesting writing.

This shell reveals secrets from the deep.
I hear the ghostly love calls of Moby Dick,
the distressed voice of a weeping mermaid.
I hear the terrified cry of a sailor
being crushed by the claws of an unknown creature.
I hear the ancient groans of stranded dolphins
and caves that give away echoing secrets
of hidden treasure.

Samantha Harding

3.2 BEACH LITTER

On any beach these days there is usually rubbish to be found, some left by thoughtless visitors and some washed ashore from boats. If children are suitably equipped with gloves then a rubbish search could be organised. This can turn up a variety of interesting objects, particularly cans. Some will still look fairly new, while others will be rusted and barely identifiable. Some may be battered and split, 'peeled' open like an apple skin or flattened vertically. There may be charred wood, debris from fishing boats, lolly sticks, plastic containers and so on.

After examination, put some of the most interesting rubbish finds into a plastic sack and, keeping gloves on, ask children to reach in and pull out a piece of litter. Now ask them to explain how it came to be on the shore. There will be fairly convincing reasons for much of the material – a plastic spoon left by a picnicking family, a plastic bottle dropped overboard by someone on a passing ship, a can thrown down by a disappointed football supporter.

Next ask the children to make up fantastic stories about their items of rubbish – the crushed can was sat on by a giant or crushed in the jaws of a sea monster, a piece of wood was charred by a dragon's breath, an old comb was once the property of a mermaid, and so on. These can be extended into stories. Alternatively let children draw their objects and then mount the pictures on card alongside their two written explanations – one plausible, one fantastic.

Talk about 'beachcombers' – who they are and what they do. Read the poem by George Mackay Brown.

Beachcomber

Monday I found a boot –
Rust and salt leather.
I gave it back to the sea, to dance in.

Tuesday a spar of timber worth thirty bob.
Next winter
It will be a chair, a coffin, a bed.

Wednesday, a half can of Swedish spirits.
I tilted my head.
The shore was cold with mermaids and angels.

Thursday I got nothing, seaweed,
A whale bone,
Wet feet and a loud cough.

Friday I held a seaman's skull,
Sand spilling from it
The way time is told on Kirkyard stones.

Saturday a barrel of sodden oranges.
A Spanish ship
was wrecked last month at The Kame.

Sunday, for fear of the elders*,
I sit on my bum.
What's heaven? A sea chest with a thousand gold coins.

George Mackay Brown

elders: in certain Protestant churches, those who help the minister manage church affairs.

This poem is a mix of fantasy and reality, of humour and seriousness. Ask children which lines appeal to them. Could they write something in a similar way? Discover something each day of the week and then comment on it.

The following task makes imaginative use of the debris found on a seashore.

Fishing debris

Lesson Ten

The Sea Spirit.

Learning Objective

To write a piece of prose using adjectives, metaphors and similes.

Resources

Seashore, beach or harbour, jotters, examples of writing.

Task

The fishing fleet at Hastings is launched from the beach and there is a wealth of interesting finds on the beach near the boats – rope, fishing netting, remains of crabs and dead dogfish, some of which have dried in the sun and taken on strange contorted shapes. Someone described these nightmarish creatures as abandoned aliens!

Talk about such observations with the children and suggest how they can be worked into an imaginative piece of writing. The idea of a sea spirit could be brought to life by creating someone or something from the debris of the seashore. In preparation for the description, ask the children to make a list of all the different kinds of rubbish that is visible in and around the harbour or seashore – such as corks, plastic bottles, cuttlefish or broken lobster pots.

Back in the classroom the children can work in pairs or individually, on creating a sea spirit. The examples can be read as an introduction and as stimulus material.

Extension Activity

Spirits can be conjured up from observations at other locations – a forest, a lake, a river, park or gardens:

> The spirit of the forest wears a
> cloak of bark, her hair is tangled vines . . .

(see also Section 2 on Castles, Houses and Ancient Monuments)

Cross-curricular links

Art – the sea spirit can be created using the actual objects, if possible, found at the location. Children can work in groups, building up the spirit on the actual beach.
ICT – take photographs of the completed sea spirit as illustrations for the piece of prose.
Geography – QCA Unit 23, Investigating Coasts

Michaela's use of alliteration is impressive in her poem, as are the ways in which she links the sea spirit to the sea by means of phrases such as 'wet fish feet . . .' and 'clacking cloak of wonderful shells'. Without the immediate experience of such wonderful first-hand stimulation, it is questionable as to whether there would have been such detail in this piece.

The first line of Fidela's poem is a terrific scene setter.

Message in a Bottle

Quite frequently there are bottles to be found on the beach and it can be interesting to imagine what messages they might contain:

> To whoever finds this note,
>
> I am your friend, left on a deserted island surrounded by sea. Where the dodo lived I stand, pleading for help, seeking a way off this bewildering island. At night I hum a lost tune that is trying to find its way home, and I sit and write this letter to you, hoping you'll come and find me soon.
>
> From Maurice

The Sea Spirit

The ghostly sea spirit has slimy seaweed hair
dripping as she rises from the rough sea
Her clacking cloak of wonderful shells
glistens in the moonlight.
With wet fish feet that slop on the shore
you can always tell it's her.
Her long pinky crab claws grind when they move
like crackling being pulled off meat.
She has a strong iron anchor attached tightly
to her thin bony legs, dragging when she tries to emerge
from the waves.
Her soft wispy voice echoes faintly
across the distant sea
whenever she decides to talk.
But remember, you never know when she'll appear
because she's out there somewhere.

Michaela Davies

The Sea Enemy

She appears in the light of a howling moon.
Her cloak is hung with pure black sea shells.
Her hair is tangled with miscellaneous seaweed.
Her feet are anchored to the deep blue sea
Her arms keep growing with three crab pincers
snipping towards you.
Her three feet are tiny and are made of fish
Her eyes are deep black pebbles, spotted.
She glides through the sea like a skilful dolphin.
She has no mouth or nose but nobody knows why.
With a click of her pincers the sea makes a wave.
Who is she? A sea enemy?

Fidela Jones

Mermaids

Everyone is fascinated by the notion of mermaids. Do they or don't they exist?

Lesson Eleven

Ten Things Found in a Mermaid's Purse.

Learning Objective

To write a list poem using adjectives and similes.

Resources

A seashore, copy of 'The Forsaken Merman' by Matthew Arnold, *The Little Mermaid* by Hans Christian Andersen (can be read online at: www.candlelightstories.com/storypage), *The Water Babies*, by Charles Kingsley (can be read online at: www.pagebypagebooks.com/Charles_Kingsley). Children's poem. An excellent resource book for work on the seashore is *The Mermaid's Purse* by Ted Hughes (Faber & Faber). This contains poems about an array of seashore creatures including a mermaid!

Task

As you walk down by the seashore, keep looking for interesting objects that have been discarded. Imagine that these have been forgotten and left by mermaids returning to the sea. Jot them down to use later. For example:

the whitest pebble ever seen
unusually shaped shells, a pearl from an oyster,
half a comb, a plastic bottle,
a cork, broken netting, frayed rope . . .

Back in the classroom, the children can work in pairs, using the notes they made at the location, and write a list poem. Use adjectives and similes to describe the objects (see above examples).

Extension Activity

The following paragraph could be used to set the scene for a piece of creative writing about a mermaid who appears quite suddenly just as the sun is setting.

I was sitting quietly on the beach at (insert your location). It seemed to me that the shimmering of the setting sun had created a golden path stretching out to the mysteries of the sea. I yawned, dusted off the sand and took one last look as the sun slipped beneath the waves. Suddenly, the peace was shattered by the crash of a large body leaping from the waves. Was it a porpoise or a whale or a dolphin? Water glittered off shining scales and I could see a large tail flicking through water. I shaded my eyes against the last rays of the sun and then gasped in amazement at what I saw. The creature had a long silver-green tail, rather like a large fish. The upper part of its body was that of a young girl whose blonde hair cascaded down. A mermaid! It was not possible, for they were creatures of the imagination. It couldn't be real! I rubbed my eyes and peered through open fingers. She was now a little closer and looking at me with the hint of sadness on her face. Was that a tear I saw or merely a droplet of seawater in the corner of her eye? With a gentle swish of her tail she swam closer to where I was standing. To my great surprise she spoke . . .

A whole class shared piece of writing could be written after brainstorming ideas about where the mermaid was going, why she had come to the surface, what words she spoke, and so on. You could begin like this:

She told me in a soft voice that her name was . . .
and that she lived deep in the ocean between . . . (insert your location)

Cross-curricular Links

Art – use pastels to create a drawing of a mermaid.
ICT – log on to the web sites mentioned in the resources, to read the two stories online. A general search for 'mermaids' brought up a fascinating collection of sites and stories which may need teacher intervention and vetting beforehand!

Ten Things found in a Mermaid's Purse

1. Half a comb for her golden hair.
2. A fragment of broken mirror for admiring herself.
3. Several dead fish for repairing her scales.
4. The chewed end of a pencil.
5. Some frayed rope, from a lobster pot.
6. A cuttlefish bone to file her long nails.
7. A golden shell, as yellow as the sun.
8. Corks to decorate her home beneath the waves.
9. A pearl from an oyster, so perfectly formed.
10. The whitest pebble you have ever seen.

Georgia, Emma and Amy

3.3 CAVES

Caves are mysterious places. They often have a history too.

Lesson Twelve

What Lies Within?

Learning Objective

To invent calligrams and a range of shape poems, and careful presentation. To use metaphors and personification to write a piece of prose.

Resources

Caves, seashore, examples of writing, jotters, the Internet, local history books.

Task

Caves are dark, spooky places, where anything could happen. As you enter the cave, carefully, feel the atmosphere and let your imagination run away with you. Jot down any observations, feelings or sounds to use later in your creative writing. Stephen made some notes while visiting a cave in Hastings:

> The dingy, darkened light of the cave,
> A ghostly feel,
> deep caverns,
> layers of rock from distant times . . .

Back at school, try presenting your ideas in a shape poem.

As an alternative, imagine the cave is a mouth, poised ready to swallow anything or anybody who dares to enter. Use your notes to help you bring the cave to life. Try to personify the cave and include how the cave must feel when noisy feet dislodge pebbles and inquisitive hands examine its slimy walls.

Here they come, pencils poised and
ready to make marks in their books.
I wish they'd take care.
Their loud voices and heavy feet echo
and vibrate around my delicate infrastructure.
One huge gulp and I could swallow them whole,
they'd be lost for ever, in my dark, deep caverns and
tunnels . . .

I got another tattoo yesterday, from a boy whose name is Jack. He put it on
with a flint stone. I've got more than fifty tattoos now and they're ruining my
natural surroundings . . . I wish kids would just admire me, not destroy me.

Extension Activity

Use the Internet, local history books and the library to research the smuggling activities of your particular location. Hastings, for example, holds a wealth of stories about smugglers and the Revenue Men who tried to prevent their activities. There were huge numbers of people involved in smuggling in the years between 1740 and 1830. Even the Vicar of All Saints Church turned a blind eye to the kegs of brandy stored in his church.

Cross-curricular Links

Geography – QCA Unit 23, Investigating Coasts.
ICT – use the Internet to search for information about famous smugglers.

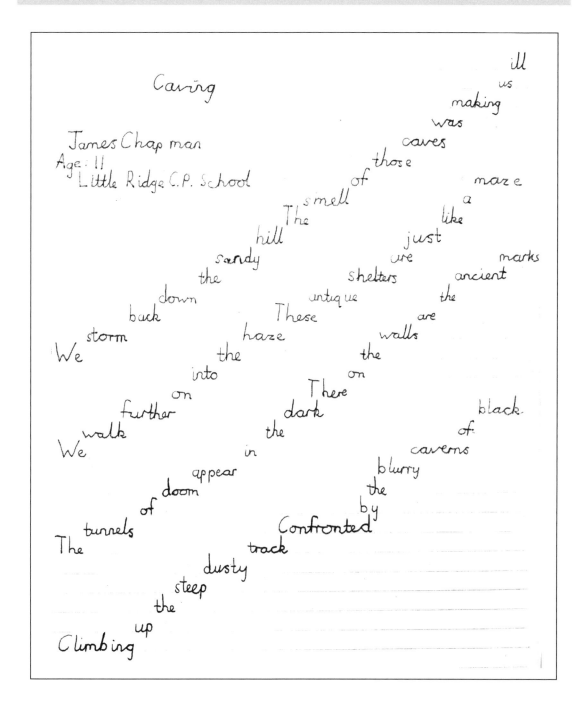

3.4 FISHING BOATS AND FISH

In a fishing fleet there is always activity of one sort or another. The boats are being prepared for a fishing trip or returning from one. Hastings has the biggest fleet of beach-launched fishing boats in Britain and it is fascinating to see how the boats enter and leave the water. It wasn't until the late 1930s that the fishermen started to use their own motor winches. Prior to that the boats were drawn up onto the beach by horse-turned capstans.

It is tempting to imagine the sort of stories that these boats could tell.

> If these fishing boats could tell a story,
> they would tell of their expeditions to far off places,
> they would tell of disturbing tragedies and exciting adventures.
> If these fishing boats could talk,
> they would tell us if there really is a paradise
> and if all that talk of beautiful mermaids
> with long golden glistening hair
> is really true.
> If only these fishing boats could tell their stories.
>
> Stacey

Suggest that children collect the names of fishing boats and to think about why they might have been given these names. At Hastings, one boat is called *Jackelly*, perhaps after a husband and wife, Jack and Kelly. It would be interesting to speculate who they are and to write something of their history. Are they still together? If they parted would the boat need to be renamed? Other boats are *Bloodaxe*, *Janet*, *Joycey*, *Valiant*, *Rosie*, *Hope* and *Ajax*. Perhaps this might also be a good time to wonder about the strangest things that fishing boats have ever trawled up in their nets. Some of the fishermen might well be willing to talk about this. Their interviews could be written out and may well provide material for stories.

Fish caught by fishing boats are often sold nearby at a fish market. Here there will probably be boards where the day's catch is chalked up. Suggest that children note down the names of some of the fish with a view to using them in their writing:

Dover sole, rainbow trout, lemon sole, cod cutlet, scotch hake, halibut, fresh haddock, plaice fillets, sea bass, fresh coley, herrings, salmon steaks, whole salmon, fresh tuna, dressed crabs, king prawns, crab sticks, fresh sardines, local whelks, brill octopus, monkfish, swordfish, squid.

Encourage children to be silly with language and to pursue an idea to ridiculous lengths. Read them the following poem as possible inspiration:

Dressed Crabs

What do crabs wear when they're dressed,
do we see them in suits and ties,
do the ladies all wear ball gowns
and carefully make up their eyes?

Do they stand in front of a mirror
and reckon they look pretty neat
do they wear stiletto heels
with toes that pinch their feet?

And when they're dressed to kill
where do you think they go?
Are they off to a high class party
or a seat at a West End show?

No, crabs have only one destination,
a cold hard fishmonger's slab,
that's the place you need to look
to spot the well-dressed crab.

Brian Moses

Some children will quickly catch on to the idea:

How Does a Monkfish Pray?

Does it go to a monastery?
Does it make a vow of silence?
Does it wear a long brown robe?
Does it study a holy book?
Does it make fish sacrifices?

I'll ask it next time I see it!

Andrew Lee

Use some of the names in a fish rap and develop a chorus:

Wrap it up with chips,
wrap it up with chips.
Open up your mouth
and put it past your lips.

Next try adding verses:

> Multi-coloured rainbow trout,
> try jellied eels and spit them out.
>
> Skates skate from rock to rock
> but can they skate around the block?

Children can have great fun with these ideas and perform their raps to different classes back at school. With a rap, of course, it doesn't matter too much if the rhymes aren't always exact ones. Provided that the words selected sound good when read aloud, it won't matter too much if half-rhymes or near rhymes are included. Encourage children to try hard to keep the rhythm going once it is established. No instruments are needed initially, just tap hands on a surface for the beat. Afterwards experiment with tambours, shakers, drums, etc. Rappers should always remember, however, that a too enthusiastic use of instruments will result in the words being obscured. The words are important and must not be obliterated!

Across the road from the fish market in Hastings is the Mermaid Restaurant. This could also be seen as a fun subject for a rap (also Neptune's Castle a little further along). Most seaside towns will have places with names such as these.

Learn to cook the Mermaid way!

The Mermaid Restaurant Rap

(Chorus)
At the Mermaid Restaurant
the mermen serve you what you want.
The mermaids serve it up all day,
the price is always low to pay.

There's jellied eels, there's smoked haddock,
the smell of crabs ready to cook.

Dressed crabs are the speciality
the food is beyond reality.

The soup of the day is smoked stingray.
Learn to cook the mermaid way!

(Chorus)

Stephen Mitchell, Michael McHugh and Joe Lamb

The Mermaid Restaurant could well provide further inspiration for writing. Ask children to design menus to show what is on offer. Can they think up slogans to attract diners to the restaurant? Could they script a 60-second radio advertisement to tempt listeners into making a booking?

3.5 SEAGULLS

Seagulls are never far from a seaside location. They are often reviled by local residents for their noisy, dirty habits. Children could interview people and ask for their opinions on the gulls. Try to find a place where gulls gather and observe their actions. Consider whether they plan their days or whether their actions are quite spontaneous.

Lesson Thirteen

Dear Diary . . .

Lesson objective

To write a first person account – in diary format.

Resources

Seashore, beach or harbour, jotters, examples of prose, *Jonathan Livingston Seagull*, by Richard Bach.

Task

Observe gulls in flight. Note how they are using the air currents to help them fly and search for food. Jot down adjectives that describe their movements, their communications to each other and their appearance. Make a note of the various types of birds seen, to use in a database.

Pair up and think about writing a diary entry for gull activities. Jot down some ideas while on location, ready to use back in the classroom.

Explain that in writing a diary, the children are writing in the first person, or in this instance, the first gull! Imagine how you would spend your day. Try to include some of the adjectives and observations you noted while at the beach.

Read *Jonathan Livingston Seagull* as a stimulus for writing.

Extension Activity

Read *Jonathan Livingston Seagull*, by Richard Bach. Write a review of the book and why you would or would not recommend it.

Cross-curricular Links

ICT – use the Internet to research different species of sea birds. Make a database of all the various seabirds spotted at your location.

Art – sketch gulls in different flying positions. (Look at the book by Richard Bach.)

Dear diary,

Today I'm doing everyday things again, just swooping around, eating fish and bread, you know like normal. I was thinking of going to France today, but I don't think I will now, the wind's changed my mind. And anyway it would be minus 3 degrees. So I think I'll just hang around here instead.

Dear diary,

Today I did the most exciting thing ever, I hitched a ride on an open top double decker bus, and guess what? You got it! Someone left the remains of a Big Mac on a seat so I had a great feast, I wonder what I'll do tomorrow.

Philippa McCall

3.6 OBSERVATION POINT

Try to find a high place where children can look down at the seaside area from above. Hastings has a viewpoint called 'The Lookout' which was a meeting place for the wives of fishermen who would gather there to wait for their husbands' boats to come home safely. From the Lookout can be seen the whole of the fishing area.

At such a high point ask children to comment on what they see below them. One observation from the Lookout was that the fishing community seemed like a tiny toy town, the kind of display model that small children might play with at the 'Early Learning Centre'. Everyone was itching to reach out a giant hand and rearrange the buildings, boats and cars. Lizzy wrote about the rooftops making a pattern like stones in a graveyard. As a fishing boat headed for the beach, rising and dipping with the waves, Charlotte wrote, 'The fishing boat is stitching the water like a needle stitches cloth.'

From a high point ask children to look at the view and to describe it, using as many of their senses as they can.

Steps

From the steps I can see a life like map
with a tale to tell.
From the steps I can smell rotting fish
and the natural scent of the sea.
From the steps I can hear the squawking seagulls
and a boat which sounds like
a combine harvester in the sea.
I can imagine me down there enjoying
everything I have dreamt.
I can see a rainbow of colours surrounding me
like a paint palette.
I can smell blossoming flowers overcoming
the scent of fish.
I can hear footsteps approaching,
I bet those feet have walked a few miles
and have a few tales to tell.
I can imagine, oh I can,
the map with no traffic,
the map without pollution,
the map without me!

Amy Hoad

3.7 MARITIME MUSEUM

A final place to visit might well be a maritime museum. This is often an excellent place to inspire writing if the weather should be bad.

The Hastings Museum tells the story of the Hastings fishing community. Originally the building was a mission church but it became a museum in 1956. It contains a 1912 sailing lugger *The Enterprise* and children can be questioned as to how the boat was brought into the museum. (The real answer is that about a third of the southern wall was pulled down and then rebuilt once the boat was inside but children will probably have far more interesting theories!)

The boat is a lovely focal point for writing as children are allowed on deck and can imagine the pitch and heave of the vessel in stormy seas:

The Boat

The rough waves crash against the strong hull,
Thunder rumbles around us like an angry demon about to shout.
Lightning flashes, lighting up the whole sky.
The boat rocks, tumbles – is this the end?

way
this   and
thrash   that
We   way.

Water splashes up the side, covering the deck in a
coating of salty foam.
Shouting echoes surround me, as the captain gives orders.
It's what fishermen have terrifying nightmares about,
It's a storm at sea.
But I'm tired of dreaming about the thrill of sailing,
I will leave this boat to rest in peace.

Stacey Cummins

On any visit to a maritime museum ask the children to find an object to inspire a story or a poem. The Shipwreck Centre and Maritime Museum at Bembridge on the Isle of Wight has a rather bizarre merman creature, and all kinds of theories can be put forward as to what this creature might be.

In Hastings Museum, Stephen found a photograph of a German U-boat that had run aground on Hastings beach in 1919. He was very excited by this picture and rapidly started composing a story about the boat. After a while he decided to write a poem instead. He chose to use a strict rhyme, line 1 rhyming with line 3, and 2 with 4, and although this isn't always completely successful, the third verse is a really skilful piece of work.

The U-Boat

As the people piled onto the beach,
A German U-boat ran aground.
The boat was out of people's reach
Until they heard the telling sound.

A great excitement over the U-boat,
They all were to go aboard.
The rejoicing on a happy note,
the boat to be explored.

They saw the dreadful war re-played,
The holograms of the dead,
The millions of deaths, just orders obeyed,
and the blood the mariners shed.

The sound of guns filled the hull,
The sound of bones being chipped,
Shatters of a mariner's skull,
The boat became a crypt.

Stephen Mitchell

Laura wrote about a ship in the bottle that she'd noticed:

The Ship

The sailors are stuck to the spot.
I feel sorry for the man who is climbing the rigging
and the one in the crow's nest,
he is forever stuck looking at the glass horizon.

The captain is looking through a telescope
but he still didn't see the giant hand that grabbed them,
the hand that put them into this bottle
where they are trapped for ever.

What are their tiny brains thinking
Or are they frozen for ever too?
Do they want a storm to wash them back to sea?
Or are they content with their still life?

Only sailors can answer these questions,
miniature ones at that,
so I think I'll leave it up to you.
If you find out, tell me.

Laura Martin

Museums will contain many items that may prove inspirational for poetry or prose. Again in Hastings, a huge wooden chest set two boys off on a story about smuggling. Where did the chest come from? It was a gift from an old sea dog, or it was hauled up from the sea bed in a fishing boat's nets are two possible answers. Elsewhere in the museum is a huge stuffed albatross with a two-metre wingspan, some barnacle encrusted anchors and Biddy the Tubman's Tub. Biddy was a Hastings character who performed tricks in a round tub while floating in the sea.

3.8 THE SEASIDE IN WINTER

Much location writing tends to be done in summer but different times of the year can promote interesting contrasts. This is especially evident in a seaside town which really does exhibit two faces – the crowded summer scene and the deserted winter picture. Below are Gary's observations of a seaside resort in winter, followed by his completed poem.

windy promenade, pier closed, silent arcades, lonely people, rough sea crashing against the breakwater, chilly, disintegrating

I walk along
the wind swept promenade,
a few lonely figures,
people who have lost
their smiles.
The bleak pier
and the arcades
out of business.
Silent,
lonely.
Rough sea
as it crashes
against the breakwater.
It seems like the town
is disintegrating.
A chilled place.

Gary

4 Countryside

Wherever children live and go to school, there is a good chance that there will be some countryside nearby. A visit could be planned around a variety of different aspects to encourage a range of responses.

Perhaps there is a particular viewpoint that might prove a starting place, followed by visits to a river, pond, wood, thicket or farm.

Ask the children to sketch their impressions in words, recording how the place makes them feel, or what particular parts of the landscape remind them of.

4.1 RIVERS AND STREAMS

The image of a meandering river as a snake may be an obvious one, but the art of the writer is to take something that is commonplace and give it a new twist. Instead of simply,

the river looks like a snake . . .

Matthew writes:

Looking down on the river, twirling about,
Laying down a blue snake on the huge fields.

Groups of children can observe the water flow in a river or stream and note down words to describe what they see and hear . . . the water rippling. flowing furiously, gyrating, mysteriously rushing, forming mini-waterfalls, rapids, flickering sunlight dancing, flashes of silver, etc.

Children can also look for evidence of creatures that live along the banks of the stream – holes in the bank, a twig dam, prints in mud. What might these creatures be?

What has happened at the stream over the years. Where does it flow to?

Lesson Fourteen

The Gurgling Stream.

Learning Objectives

(a) To write a poem that uses metaphors, similes and alliteration to create effects.
(b) To design an advertisement for a newspaper, advertising a river creature's home for sale.

Resources

Copy of 'Our Ditch' by Brian Moses, examples of other poems written by children, jotters, a stream or ditch, examples of advertisements of houses for sale, 'Stream Story' by Paul Bright.

Tasks

A poem about the movement of the water could be composed featuring children's observations. Some children might like to tell the story of the stream. Decide what happens to it on its journey from source to sea. Read 'Stream Story' as an example. Another idea is to think about what has happened at the stream over the years. Read 'Our Ditch' by Brian Moses.

Differentiated Task

Display a chart depicting the different sections of a river from its source to the sea. Children can add words and illustrations to the chart.

Extension Activity

Children can look at examples of estate agents' advertisements and try to compose an advert for a stream creature's home. How would you make a hole for a water rat sound attractive to potential customers?

Cross-curricular Links

Geography – QCA Unit 14, Investigating Rivers.
Art – design a new home for one of the stream creatures.
Music – compose a piece of music, based on the sounds heard while observing the river/stream/ditch.

Our Ditch

I sat and thought one day
of all the things we'd done
with our ditch; how we'd jumped across
at its tightest point, till I slipped
and fell, came out smelling,
then laid a pole from side to side,
dared each other to slide along it.
We fetched out things that others threw in,
lobbed bricks at tins, played Pooh sticks.
We buried stuff in the mud and the gunge
then threatened two girls with a ducking.
We floated boats and bombed them,
tiptoed along when the water was ice
till something began to crack, and we scuttled back.
We borrowed mum's sieve from the baking draw,
scooped out tadpoles into a jar
then simply forgot to put them back.
(We buried them next to the cat).
Then one slow day in summer heat
we followed our ditch to where it began,
till ditch became stream, and stream
fed river, and river sloped off to the sea.
Strange, we thought, our scrap of water
growing up and leaving home,
roaming the world and lapping
at distant lands.

Brian Moses

Stream Story

Stream in the hillside,
Burbling, trickling,
Splashing through my fingers,
Tugging and tickling.

Tumbling to the valley,
Gurgling, growing,
Pooh-stick highway,
Filling and flowing.

Bustling with water life,
Flourishing, thriving,
On water, underwater,
Swimming and diving.

Now a mighty waterway,
Ships in motion,
Taking all the traffic
To the great, grey ocean.

Paul Bright

Suggest that children compose prayers to the river from fishermen or sailors whose lives are connected with the water. Their concerns will be for safety, asking the river to stay calm, and possibly hoping that fish will be plentiful.

River who can be as gentle as a lamb
or as rough as a lion.

River whose power can sink boats
and drown people.

River whose rippling beauty flows
gently to your father the sea.

Launch my boat with your mighty waves,
push me to the sea.

Pull fish to my net and then
I will ask no more of you.

Simon

Talk about personification. As the children observe, can they give the river a voice? Let it speak, complain, whine or boast of its power:

I am the power of the river.
I can flood towns and villages.

I am the power of the river,
I can wreck unwary tugboats.

Fill a cup with me
and I will jingle and jerk out of it.

Consider too, the power of a waterfall. Robert arranged his observations into the shape of a waterfall.

The Waterfall
roars
as
it
Comes
down
the
cliff
bringing
rocks.
It
rustles
and
when
it
hits
the
bottom
it goes
splash!

Robert Perfitt 7yrs

If children find it difficult to start writing, suggest that they begin with some questions. These may then become part of the writing itself. Here, John found a daisy growing in a place where a river regularly floods and it prompted this observation:

> Daisy, how do you survive the floods
> when your roots are so shallow
> and your flower so delicate?

What about creatures that live in a river or stream? If there are ducks, try to observe how they float in the water and how they move when they're on land. Ask children to try to describe how they walk – waddling like marching soldiers, follow m'leader style; and how they communicate – 'blabbering on'.

Give the ducks names and identities – Ding and Dong, Doreen and David, Dolores and Doug. Point out and encourage the alliterative effects in the names.

Were there creatures that used to live in the river but have left now? Louise learnt about the otters that used to live in the River Cuckmere.

> **The Otters' Spirit**
>
> The otters went but their spirit stayed.
> You can see they used to be here.
> The wind forms a shape of an otter's head.
> I miss the otters so much.
> The reed birds sing and flutter but I still miss them.
> Who knows where they've gone?
> You can just feel that they've been here.
> The river runs silently, no splashes.
> maybe they'll come back,
> I hope so.
>
> Louise Read

4.2 HILLS

Before any visit to write on location, it is necessary to find out something about the place to be visited. When climbing a hill, pause at various stages and relate a little of the history of the place. These ideas will be picked up by the children and can become the focus of shared class writing around the starting point of 'This Hill . . .' or 'These Hills . . .'

These hills have seen oak trees being cleared,
Stone Age men fashioning tools from flint.
These hills have seen dug-out canoes being paddled up river,
Turf cut to the shape of a horse
by Victorians on picnics.
These hills have heard the clip clop of hooves
replaced by the rumble of cars.
These hills have seen hang-gliders butterflying across the sky.
They have been grazed by generations of cattle,
cropped by sheep, mined with rabbit tunnels.
These hills have seen smugglers' boats
sailing past the excise men.
They have seen funeral ceremonies.
and wagon walkers on the White Way . . .
They have heard the bombers drone by
when the world was at war.
These hills have been here for all of these things
And will be for evermore.

Climbing a very steep hill such as High and Over in the Sussex Downs can promote some interesting rhythmic pieces that can then be set to a percussion beat:

High and Over,
High and Over
We went climbing on
High and Over,
It was wet and slippery,
someone fell over
on High and Over,
High and Over . . .

Then playing with the 'Over' rhyme other verses can be added:

Thought we could see
as far as Dover.

Someone came by
with a dog called Rover.

Once these hills
were walked by a drover.

or alternatively:

> Right to the top,
> right to the top,
> we climbed this hill
> right to the top,
> we ran out of hill
> so we had to stop,
> right to the top,
> right to the top.

In any presentation of a rhythmical piece of writing it is important that instruments don't obscure the words. Tone of voice, clarity of diction, emphasis, speed of reading – all these factors need to be right for an audience to gain maximum enjoyment.

Who lies here?

Burial Mounds

These can sometimes be found on hillsides and it is interesting to speculate about them. Who is buried under the burial mound? Is it a warrior chieftain from long ago or is the grave marking a more recent and sinister event? If so, did anyone see what happened? Were the trees or the clouds or the sky witness to what happened?

Ask children to consider the life and death of the grave's occupant. Try and avoid Dracula/Zombie clichés and encourage an historical perspective, a mystical feel. If this is the grave of a mysterious warrior, write about him, find a picture of him in a history book, give him a name, a family, a place to live. What were his weapons?

Design a gravestone for the grave's occupant. What would be inscribed on it? Write an epitaph: 'Here lies . . .'

Or begin a story in this way:

> 'Stop walking over my grave,' boomed a voice. ' Do you not know that you're walking on the grave of . . .'

The following example was written after examining a burial mound on the South Downs.

Treasure

Have you taken my treasure,
My precious treasure?
Have you taken my gold,
My lovely gold?
Have you taken my silver,
My shiny silver?
Have you taken my soul,
My important soul?

Yes, I have taken your treasure,
Your precious treasure.
Yes, I have taken your gold,
Your lovely gold.
Yes, I have taken your silver,
Your shiny silver.
Yes, I have taken your soul,
Your important soul
AND I SHALL KEEP IT!

Georgina Beavis

Hill Figures: White Horses, Giants etc.

There are many white horses to be found on hillsides in Wiltshire and at least eight others outside of Wiltshire (see Section 7, Resources, for exact locations).

On any visit children should be asked to speculate as to why these figures have been cut into hillsides. There are various theories about the Uffington White Horse in Oxfordshire which is thought to date from the Bronze Age. These include religious origins, a local tribe's emblem, and a gift to either the horse goddess Rhiannon or the sun god Belinos (Belenus).

Some horses, like the one at Litlington in Sussex, were cut more recently, in this instance in February 1924, to replace one that previously existed on that site.

Quite often there are local legends associated with hill figures and these should be explored. Maybe the horse has special powers. Maybe it is a good luck charm for the area. What would happen if it disappeared?

Children can stretch their imaginations when writing about a white horse. Sometimes it is sufficient just to lie back on a hillside and dream, like Harriet.

Chalk Horse

Chalk horse, chalk horse
Carry me away
Over the land and far away.
Into the middle of the forest where it is
dark and beautiful.
Chalk horse, chalk horse,
Carry me away
Into the sky where we can stay.

Harriet Baille

Sun Horse, Moon Horse

On the mound you lie,
Head tilted towards the sun and moon,
A dream-like stallion,
Dominant and powerful.
Listening intently to the far-off call of a war horn,
You seem to be waiting,
Waiting for some mystery to come bubbling up
From the earth's crust
Like an unknown force,
Bringing passion, fury and a burning supremacy
To this
Sun horse, Moon horse.

Rebecca Martin

In Sussex the Litlington White Horse looks across the Cuckmere Valley where there is a legend about two giants. They lived on different hills each side of the valley and were forever arguing and throwing missiles at each other. The best known of these giants is the Long Man of Wilmington which stands 273 feet tall on the side of Windover Hill, near Wilmington. His opponent was the giant who lived on Firle Beacon. The legend states that the Long Man eventually fought with the Firle giant and lost. The outline on Windover Hill is reputed to be the spot where he died. Another view is that the Long Man is standing in a doorway between one world and the next.

Legends such as these abound throughout Britain and children can be asked to retell them in their own language or to write different versions:

The Giant

The giant will come,
He will take our special horse,
Ride it away, come back and put it in a different place.
The giant will come,
He will leave big footsteps,
He will make a thunder noise.
The giant will come.
We are lucky to have protective houses,
So he will not stamp on us.
The giant will come,
The giant is coming!
Boom! Boom! Boom!
Gallop! Gallop! Gallop!

Laura Hunter

Giants

Once upon a time there were giants:
Two lazy giants
sitting on hilltops,
two noisy giants
loudmouthing each other all night,
keeping the nearby villages awake.
Two rowdy giants
rolling rocks down valleys
like bowling balls,
hurling insults
scrawled on boulders:
CRASH!
'Pea-Brain'
SMASH!
'Big Nut'
THUMP!
'Daft Lump'
And if you were unlucky enough
to stumble into the flight path
of boulders from angry giants
you'd be bowled over,
squashed flat,
lost from sight,
unless by chance some giant
picked up that boulder again
and finding something messy beneath
wiped you off on the grass . . .

But of course there wouldn't have been
so many broken bones
if only these two giants
had had mobile phones!

Brian Moses

What
would we
miss if
there were
no trees?

4.3 TREES

We tend to take trees for granted. Ask children to imagine a world without trees. What would we miss if there were no trees?

> The tree answered back, 'Well there will be no shade for you to
> rest in. And there will be no birds on my branches to sing for you.'

Consider how trees become good friends to everything living in them or on them. Use the poem by Brian Moses, 'Make Friends with a Tree', for group performance. It should be recited with great gusto, particularly the chorus. Individual children could read the verses but the choruses should be for everyone. Try hand-clapping on the chorus or using percussion instruments to assist the rhythm.

Make Friends with a Tree

Give a tree a squeeze,
give a tree a hug,
join in celebration
with every bird and bug,

with every bat and badger,
with beetles and with bees,
a new year's resolution,
show kindness to the trees.

Make friends with a tree,
make friends with a tree,
hug a tree, go on show it
you really care, let a tree know it.

Make friends with a tree,
make friends with a tree.

Trees are always homes
to every sort of creature.
In a flat and empty landscape
a tree is a special feature.

Trees can be deciduous,
pine trees are coniferous,
but trees will never hurt you
no tree is carnivorous!

So treat a tree politely,
show it you're sincere.
Long after we have disappeared,
trees will still be here.

Make friends with a tree,
make friends with a tree,
hug a tree, go on show it
you really care, let a tree know it.
Make friends with a tree,
make friends with a tree.

Snuggle up to a sycamore,
cuddle up to a pine
wrap your arms around an oak,
enjoy a joke with a lime.

A tree will always listen,
tell your troubles to a tree.
To the mystery of life
an ash may hold the key.

So don't be abrupt with a birch,
don't try to needle a pine.
don't interrupt a horse chestnut,
don't give a tree a hard time.

Make friends with a tree,
make friends with a tree,
hug a tree, go on show it
you really care, let a tree know it.
Make friends with a tree,
make friends with a tree.

A tree is a living thing,
it's not just a lump of wood.
Trees in Sherwood Forest
know all about Robin Hood.

A tree can tell us stories,
a tree knows history,
so in this world of fake and sham
let's celebrate truth in a tree.

Make friends with a tree,
make friends with a tree,
hug a tree, go on show it
you really care, let a tree know it.
Make friends with a tree,
make friends with a tree.

Brian Moses

Are there any fallen trees in the area? Children could try to imagine what it would be like on a night of powerful storms. If a tree came down in high winds, what would be its thoughts and feelings? Does it feel helpless, ashamed, upset, frightened? And at night, in the darkness, what would be a tree's dreams?

Lesson Fifteen

The Dreaming Tree.

Learning Objective

To write a poem based on personal or imagined experience. List brief phrases and words, experiment by trimming or extending sentences; experiment with powerful and expressive words.

Resources

Examples of poems, an open space, park or public gardens, trees, jotters.

Task

All trees are different, some are a very unusual shape. Try to look for a tree that seems out of place, compared with the majority.
Think about what this tree might be thinking or dreaming of doing, if it were planted somewhere else. Why does it look out of place? Where should it be?
Note down some ideas about where this tree wishes it was and what it would do there. Does it dream of walking, talking, or going on holiday to a tropical island?

Extension Activities

Children might like to think of a theme, for example, dancing, and write about various types of dances that the tree might dream of (see examples of poems, below).

Differentiated Task

Children could use a word bank on the computer to help them construct their poem. A writing template could be used:

> The tree dreams . . .
> It dreams of . . .
> The tree dreams . . .
> It dreams of . . .

Words from the word bank are inserted to complete the sentences.

Cross-curricular Links

QCA Science, QCA Unit 4b – Habitats.

Examples of Poems

This poem has a theme of dancing running through it.

> A tree dreams of dancing
> of picking up its roots
> and pirouetting like a ballerina.
> The tree dreams of a disco,
> of wearing platforms and a mini-skirt.
> She dreams of tap-dancing,
> of clicking her shoes to the beat.
> She dreams of partying
> all night long.

Suggest that older children stretch their imaginations but stick to the idea that they have written in their first line so that the poem develops from this, i.e. everything in the above poem is about dancing.

This tree is dreaming of going on holiday to somewhere warm!

> The tree dreams of tropical islands,
> of sandy beaches with gentle waves
> and dolphins playing chase.
> It dreams of visiting relations
> and telling them how rainy Guernsey is.
> It dreams of sunbathing in a tiny bikini
> And scoffing down coconut milk.
> It dreams of swimming in the sea
> and snorkelling beneath the reefs.

Alternatively let the children give a tree lots of dreams. Put the ideas together in a poem for choral speaking.

A tree dreams
A tree dreams
Tell me what does a tree dream?

It dreams of dancing with wolves
In a moonlit meadow land.
It dreams of running with cheetahs
On the scorching desert sand.

It dreams of screaming at rooks,
'Just get out of my branches'.
It dreams of riding wild mustangs
On the crazy Texas ranches.

It dreams of flying with birds
In the starry midnight skies.
It dreams of eating with elephants
And juicy apple pies.

A tree dreams
A tree dreams
Tell me what does a tree dream?

It dreams of playing football
In England, France and Spain.
It dreams of walking mountains
And racing over plains.

It dreams of singing with pop stars
And getting to Number One.
It dreams of talking with lions
In Africa under the sun.

It dreams of smelling the flowers
It's lived with for so long.
It dreams of eating pancakes
In a café with King Kong.

A tree dreams
A tree dreams
Tell me what does a tree dream?

A tree dreams
A tree dreams
Tell me
    what
        does
            a tree
                dream?

(Group poem, Isle of Wight)

Ask children to imagine what it would be like to be a tree. Refer them to Grandmother Willow in the Disney film *Pocahontas* who pulls up her roots so that John Smith's friends trip over them and flicks her vines to send them away. Would the children be mischievous as trees, or demanding, or vain, or cooperative, or what?

If I were a tree
and children came to fiddle with me,
I think I'd stick out my roots
and trip them up.
What fun it would be if I were a tree.

If I were a tree
and people left me alone,
I'd make myself a better looking cedar tree
so people would come and look at me,
If I were a tree ...

If I were a tree ...

Emma

In Lydia Fulleylove's poem below, two trees growing where countryside meets sea are having a conversation.

Palm Tree Talk

'Listen,' said the tallest palm,
'There's a storm blowing in.'
'How do you know?' said the smallest palm.
'I can hear nothing.'

'Look,' said the tallest palm,
'The wind has cuffed the waves.'
'What do you mean?' said the smallest palm.
'I can see nothing.'

'Feel,' said the tallest palm.
'The leaf rattler, the trunk bender.'
'Shall we sing?' said the smallest palm.
'Shall we dance?'

Lydia Fulleylove

Children might like to make up their own conversations between trees. Perhaps there are trees growing side by side that don't get on with each other. What sort of things might annoy trees? What would they complain about?

4.4 FORESTS

Lesson Sixteen

Lost in the Forest.

Learning Objective

To write an extended story, worked on over time, on a theme identified in reading and on location.

Resources

A wood, forest or small copse; a copy of *Little Red Riding Hood, Hansel and Gretel* or *Snow White and the Seven Dwarves*; Chapter 2 of *The Hobbit* – 'Roast Mutton'; Book 1 of *The Lord of the Rings – The Fellowship of the Rings*; *Harry Potter and The Philosopher's Stone* by J. K. Rowling; jotters.

Task While on Location

As the children are walking near or through a group of trees or even a small wood, encourage them to jot down how they feel. Do the trees make them feel scared, frightened, worried, at ease, peaceful?
What colours can they see? Describe the shapes:

Long, slender branches, thinning to delicate twigs.
Leaves – shades of greens.
Bark – lichen covered, mossy, slimy, old and wrinkled.

These notes will be used in their stories, back in the classroom.

Task in Class

Read the description of The Forbidden Forest from *Harry Potter and The Philosopher's Stone* and the description of the old forest near the start of the chapter 'The Old Forest' from Book 1 of Tolkein's *The Lord of the Rings*. You might like to read the other stories mentioned above under Resources as well. Using their notes made while on location, plan a story entitled 'Lost in the Forest'. This story can be written over several sessions. For example:

1. Plan story, using the school planning sheet. Write introduction. Children could read out their work.
2. Write first chapter – beginning.
3. Write second chapter – middle.
4. Write third chapter – end, conclusion.

Invite the children to suggest ideas for the story. How did they, or another character become lost?

How do they feel? What do they see, hear, imagine as they wander through the wood? What happens? (Chapter 2)

How is it resolved, end? (Chapter 3)

Differentiation

Children might be paired, so they can work together on their story. The top group would be expected to write at least three chapters, whereas the lower group might aim for just one.

Cross-curricular Links

Art – a class frieze of the woods can be painted, or sketched. Individual tree shapes can be drawn to resemble human forms – personify the tree.
Science – linked to QCA Unit on Habitats.
Drama – see extension activitiy.

Extension Activity

Read part of Chapter 2 from *The Hobbit*, where the three trolls are sitting around their fire moaning about their meal.

Divide the class into groups of four and ask them to choose who will be Bilbo and who will be the trolls. Read the section one more time, then ask the children to act out the scene.

Encourage them to remember some of the vocabulary the trolls used. Give them a few minutes to decide on their characters, before you read the passage for a third time.

While the children are listening, tell them to imagine how they would be behaving and acting as their chosen characters. Finally let them work on their sketches. They can then show each other.

(Follow-up lesson to Drama)

Lesson Seventeen

Oh No Not Roast Mutton!

Learning Objective

To prepare and write a playscript, applying conventions learned from reading and drama.

Resources

A selection of published playscripts, jotters.

Task

Look at a selection of playscripts. Discuss the way the dialogue and narration are set out on the page. Talk about how this is a different way of writing a story compared to the narrative mixed with dialogue that children are used to.

Use the group drama session as a starting point for writing a playscript that retells the scene with the trolls. The children can work in their groups, all contributing to the script. Remember to begin by listing the characters, then describe the setting. Each child can write down what they said in their sketch. Stage directions can be added afterwards, when the dialogue has been written. The group can act out what they have written, as they go along.

Cross-curricular Links

Art – draw the scene of the trolls in the woods, sitting around the fire. Paint or use pastels.

5 Parks and Gardens

Before any visit, spend time finding out what children know about parks and gardens – locally and elsewhere. Has anyone visited parks in a city such as London? 'London's parks are the lungs of the city' – do children understand what this means?

For further ideas that may be useful when visiting parks and gardens see Lesson Plans 1.5 and 4.3 on **Trees** in both 'The School Environment' and 'Countryside' Sections, Lesson Plan 4.1 on **Rivers and Streams** in the 'Countryside' chapter, and Lesson Plans 1.3, 1.4, 1.7 on **The School Pond, Walls and Hedgerows, and Flowers**, in 'The School Environment'.

5.1 THE CHANGING PARK

Lesson Eighteen

The Changing Park.

Learning Objective

To write a poem using metaphors from original ideas or from similes.

Resources

Poem by Ian Souter, 'Early Last Sunday Morning'; park/playground; jotters; the first story in *Nothing to be Afraid of* by Jan Mark.

Task

Invite the children to jot down sounds they hear as they walk around the park or gardens, such as rustling leaves on the path, distant sounds of traffic, bird song.

Ask how these sounds might differ at night. How else might the park change? Talk about the differing seasons, weather, plant and animal life. Discuss what could be seen at other times in the park – on a sunny Sunday, in drizzle or a winter's dusk. What would they hear at night?

Read Ian Souter's poem 'Early Last Sunday Morning' as a stimulus for children's own poems about changes in the park. Using some of Ian Souter's metaphors, the children could extend the lines by adding similes. For example:

'Inside we watched the trees stretch and wake'
like children getting up to the sound of the alarm clock

or

'Soon I was pointing towards a spider
that was strung on a necklace web'
like a

Differentiated Task

Children could work in different ability pairs to extend the lines in the poem. Higher ability groups could write their own poem about the changing park and include metaphors and similes. For example:

It was dusk when we entered the park,
Leaves rustled underfoot
Like hundreds of bursting bubble-wrap.
Darkness surrounded us
like a flowing cloak . . .

Read the first story in Jan Mark's book, *Nothing to be Afraid of*, where she gives places in the park names, like Leopard's Walk, or Poison Alley, and meets creatures such as the Greasy Witch and the Lavatory Demon.

Children could create strange names for places in the park they are looking round. They could develop a trail and describe the different places on the route, along with the strange people or creatures that could be found there

Extension Activity

Make a list of all the different plants and trees that grow in the park.

Why do these thrive here? Find out about other species of plants that grow in other parts of the world. Why does a cactus grow to gigantic size in the Arizona desert?

Cross-curricular Links

Art – draw pictures of the park or playground showing both day and night on the same sheet of paper. Take one of the lines in the poem by Ian Souter, for example, 'a glass of fresh air' and illustrate it. Children can have great fun with this!

IT – record sounds heard in the park. Use the Internet or online encyclopaedia to find out about the flowers and trees that are growing in the park.

Science – QCA Unit 4b, Habitats.

Early Last Sunday Morning

Early last Sunday morning
Dad said we needed a glass of fresh air
and a mouthful of greenness.
So off we slipped to the nearby park
where we crept in as soundless as snails.
Around us the day breathed air
that was as sharp as vinegar,
reminding us that winter was on its way.

Inside we watched the trees stretch and wake
while the grass stood up and shivered.
Soon I was pointing towards a spider
that was strung on a necklace web
while behind it,
the sun rolled out like a golden ball.

Dad smiled,
as the squirrel scampered from a bush
then turned to grey stone,
until with a flick of its tail
it waved goodbye and was gone.

Later as we passed the children's playground
I looked at the lonely red slide
and briefly remembered the summer days
when I flew its long slippery tongue.
But a cold wind pushed me past
until I just let the warmth in my dad's hand
lead me on home.

Ian Souter

5.2 PARK FACILITIES

Lesson Nineteen

Letters of Complaint/Encouragement.

Learning Objective

To draft and write individual, group or class letters for real purposes, for example, to complain or to praise positive developments.

Resources

Park or playground, jotters, example of letter.

Task

As they tour a park ask children to note down things that look wrong, or perhaps amenities that might be missing in the park. They should also look for positive things about the park too. They could draw up two columns for separate lists.

Observations might include too many weeds, graffiti on walls or fences, broken fence or gate, missing fence around a pond or lake, poor state of toilets, and so on. Positive developments could include refurbished cafe, safe playground, dog dirt bins, new cycle tracks, etc.

Leading on from this there could be a class discussion to decide whether the good developments outweigh the complaints. If there is still room for improvement in the park then a whole class activity might be to write a letter of complaint to the local council. Remind children how to set out a letter and that their letter should contain positive elements, as well as complaints. Use the resource letter as a guide.

Individual Task

Children can use the class example to help them to write their own letters to the council. Encourage positive comments, mention what was good about the park. Children can pair up in mixed ability pairs.

Extension Activity

Choose one or two well-written letters to send to the local newspaper. Following on from such a visit children can propose their own solutions to the problems that they note. How can the pond be kept clear of litter? What can be done about vandalism?

Cross-curricular Links

Art – design an ideal playground. Suggest the size of the play area, perhaps the size of their playground.
Science – QCA Unit 4b, Habitats.

Resource Letter

Class 9
A Primary School
West Bourne.

4.01.03.

West Bourne Council Offices
Cobbly End
West Bourne.

Dear Sir,

On Monday 1st May we went to Primrose Park. We enjoyed the new play area and the flower displays but we were upset to see lots of rubbish in the pond. We also thought that the toilets could be much cleaner than they are. We are lucky that our school is near to the park, but there were lots of younger children playing on the swings who may have needed a toilet.
Would it be possible for you to build a new toilet block please?
Thank you very much.

Yours faithfully,

Class 9

6 Further Ideas for Location Writing

6.1 BONFIRES

Watch a bonfire being built in the days leading up to 5th November. Note down all the items that you can see on the heap. Read the poem, 'The Bonfire at Barton Point' and see how a number of such items have been arranged into two verses:

> There were beehives, signboards, slats and tables,
> car tyres, a sledge and a wrecked go-cart,
> a radiogram with a case of records,
> some put-together furniture that must have pulled apart.
>
> And like patients forsaken in mid operation
> there were three piece suites in states of distress,
> gashes in sides, stuffing pulled out,
> and a huge Swiss roll of a mattress

Can children find rhythms and rhymes in the lists that they have drawn up?

Alternatively, collect words that describe what the bonfire looks/sounds/feels/ smells like from the lighting of the first match to the cold ashes when the fire has died down. A number of questions can be asked to help the children: What colours can you see? How do the flames move? What sounds does a fire make? What happens to the wood? What comes out of the top of the fire? What is left in the morning?

Fantasise about the bonfire. Why was it started? What was burnt there? Was it a dragon ? If so, what were the events leading up to the lighting of the fire?

Research Viking ship burnings. Read the last part of *Beowulf* where '. . . the Geats built a funeral pyre, hung round with helmets and shields and shining mail'.

Find something of interest in the remains of a bonfire. Look at it closely (but from a safe distance and never go into an unlit bonfire). What does it make you think of? List any ideas that spring to mind. One of these phrases or sentences about the object could then become the starting point for a poem.

Resources

Beowulf – retold by Charles Keeping, illustrated by Kevin Crossley-Holland (OUP); *Dragons – Fire Breathing Poems* by Nick Toczek (Macmillan); 'The Bonfire at Barton Point' by Brian Moses (from *Don't Look at Me in That Tone of Voice*) (Macmillan).

6.2 CHURCHYARDS AND CEMETERIES

Many fascinating details may be found in such locations. Children should find some old gravestones and examine the details on the stone. These can be used to make up a poem.

> Mary Oxley, widow of David Oxley,
> lies herself dead. An engraved cross at the top,
> a block of stone, six feet of earth, a coffin
> and then her,
> lying silently, sleeping till eternity.
> Grass shooting up, the beginnings of a tree.
> Died at Chiddingly
> March 12th 1881, aged 86 years.

Some cemeteries may have epitaphs on the gravestones and children might like to collect some of these. Epitaphs tell us about the life and times of former generations, their trades and occupations. The following is an epitaph for an angler from Ripon Cathedral in Yorkshire:

> Here lies poor, but honest Bryan Tunstall: he was a most expert angler, until
> Death, envious of his Merit threw out his line, hook'd him, and landed him here
> the 21st day of April 1790.

Children might like to try writing epitaphs of their own beginning with the words, 'Here lies . . .' Think of epitaphs for a policeman, a traffic warden, a rock star, a footballer and so on.

6.3 GARGOYLES

Gargoyles may be seen in many different places – churches, castles, old houses. Do children know what purpose they serve? Ask them to consider what the gargoyles are looking at. What have they seen over the years? Perhaps they hold conversations at night. Children could write a piece for two voices. Would they complain or boast or feel sad about themselves? Do they mind people pointing at them, laughing and calling them ugly? What has the weather done to their faces over time?

In the poem below, Lindsay makes good use of assonance – words with the same vowel sounds – 'years', 'here', 'peering' (in bold letters). This is an effective technique and one which helps to strengthen the rhythm and flow of the poem.

Gargoyle

With hideous head and **glaring** eyes
I was made to **stare** down upon all.
For **years** I have sat up **here**
Peering with my **beady** eyes way **down** on the **town**.
For **years** I have **feared** that
I should crumble and fall
hundreds of feet to the ground.
I have prayed that once I should walk
among the glamorous people,
but never was my **prayer** answered.
I **stare** into the beautiful glass window,
through the rows of polished pews.
I wish to sit there but no.
Of all the grotesque monsters
I am the worst.
I am the GARGOYLE.

Lindsay

6.4 AN EMPTY HOUSE

Visiting an empty house is particularly effective if you can arrange to visit in the evening when it is getting dark. First hold a session of spooky storytelling and then, while the children are occupied in some task downstairs, arrange for an adult to slip away and go upstairs without the children's knowledge. Then try to explain the footsteps that can be heard from upstairs!

The Bonfire at Barton Point

The bonfire at Barton Point
was a wonderful sight, a spectacular blaze,
stuff legends are made of, wicked, ace!
We were talking about it for days.

There were beehives, signboards, slats and tables,
car tyres, a sledge and a wrecked go-cart,
a radiogram with a case of records,
some put-together furniture that must have pulled apart.

And like patients forsaken in mid operation
there were three piece suites in states of distress,
gashes in sides, stuffing pulled out,
and a huge Swiss roll of a mattress.

And we knew we'd need some giant of a guy
to lord it over a pile like this,
not a wimp in a baby's pushchair
that the flames would quickly dismiss.

But on the great and glorious night
we found it hard to believe our eyes
as tilted and tumbled onto the fire
came a whole procession of guys.

Then adults took over and just to ensure
the pile of guys would really burn,
they doused the heap with paraffin
so no ghost of a guy could return.

Then matches flared, torches were lit
at several points around the fire,
till suddenly everything caught at once
and fingers of flame reached higher.

And beaming guys still peered through smoke
till the fiery serpent wrapped them round
in coils of flame, and they toppled down
to merge with the blazing mound.

With our faces scorched, we turned away,
driven back by waves of heat
till after a time the fire slumped back,
its appetite replete.

Now as long as we live we'll remember
Barton Point with its fiery display
and the charred and blackened treasures
that we pulled from the ashes next day.

Brian Moses

7 Resources

Section 2 Castles, Houses and Ancient Monuments

The following websites may be useful.

1. Castles on the web
www.castlesontheweb.com

Very comprehensive site on just about anything to do with castles, world wide. The link 'Castle Kids' is brilliant. Here you will discover online games and activities, puzzles and virtual communities of castles.

There are castle collections, castle books, a link to abbeys and churches and a section of castle glossary.

2. Castles of Britain
www.castles-of-britain.com

A site dedicated to the study and promotion of British castles. The site has a 'castle of the month' section which is quite informative. There is also a photogallery which includes over 60 different castles.The section on castle ghosts is very interesting. Did you know that a ghost from King Charles II's time browses books in the library of Arundel Castle, Sussex? He is known as the 'Blue Man'.

A dripping wet ghost haunts Scotney Castle in Kent. It is said that the man was a Revenue Officer murdered by smugglers.

Another fascinating section is Castle Trivia. At Exeter Castle in 1136, the garrison used wine to extinguish fires from a siege. One of the largest castle ruins in England is Kenilworth Castle located in Warwickshire.

3. Arundel Castle
www.castles-abbeys.co.uk/Arundel-Castle.html

All you ever need to know about Arundel Castle, West Sussex. Includes many photographs.

4. Castles of Wales
www.castlewales.com

This is a very colourful and quick-loading site, devoted to castles in Wales. It caters for Welsh language speakers as well! There is a very useful castle location map section, where if you click on part of the map of Wales, a close-up of that particular area is revealed, together with the locations of any castles in the area. The whole site includes many photographs and historical texts.

5. Dunstanburgh Castle
www.theheritagetrail.co.uk/Castles/dunstanburgh
Perched high on a cliff, Dunstanburgh Castle is now largely ruinous, although it rated at one time among the largest and grandest castles in the north of England.

6. Images of Dunstanburgh
www.ejr.ndo.co.uk

Click on the smaller images to obtain a larger one. There are links to other castles in different parts of England and Scotland.

7. Scottish Castles and Historic Houses
www.aboutscotland.com/castles/castles.html

This first page gives a choice of castles and houses to explore online. For example, Strome Castle – built by the Rosses, owned by MacDonalds and attacked by McKenzies. A sea-loch fortress on the west coast near Lochcarron.

There are many sites devoted to Hadrian's Wall. All of the following are very useful and give some super photographs and information.

8. Hadrian's Wall
www.hadrians-wall.org/homepage.htm

Hadrian's Wall is the most important monument built by the Romans in Britain.

9. The Building of Hadrian's Wall
www.aboutscotland.com/hadrian/wall.html

This site gives a map showing the length of the Wall from east to west, together with important museums and places of interest along the way.

10. Photographs of Hadrian's Wall
www.graeme-peacock.com/hadrians_wall.htm

This site has a wealth of photographs showing different views of the Wall.

11. Beautiful England
www.beautiful-england.co.uk/northumberland.htm

This particular link to Northumberland contains many images of castles, Hadrian's Wall and surrounding islands.

Section 3 The Seashore

Websites

1. Hastings Old Town
www.hastings.uk.net

Take a virtual tour of Hastings – the next best thing to actually going there. There is a super section on the Hastings fishing fleet and a collection of photographs showing the launching of a fishing boat. Typing 'beach' in the search box will reveal Hastings beach with a link to beach artist, Sid Benynon. Sid creates images on the beach using the natural colours and shapes of the pebbles as his palette.

2. Guernsey Tourist Board
www.guernseytouristboard.com

Clicking on the 'beach' link at the bottom of the page will lead you to a number of award-winning beaches in Guernsey. There is also a facility on this site to view photographs as an interactive image, giving 360 degree views.

3. Rocky seashores
www.purchon.com/ecology/rocky.htm

This is a very informative site about life below the shore line. There are some super photographs showing plant and animal life. Some of the text is quite technical, but the close-up images explain it well.

4. The Smugglers' Adventure
http://discoverhastings.co.uk/smugglers

You will need to have Flash 5 to view this brilliant site, but there is a facility to download the program from the site. Did you know that Hastings was a town full of smugglers? The old town is a warren of secret tunnels and passages, and many buildings still show signs of the smuggling past. Deep in the heart of Hastings West Hill lies the Smugglers' Adventure, acres of caverns that conceal Hastings' thrilling history of smugglers, bootleggers and warring gangs.
    This site takes you on a virtual tour of West Hill. Be prepared, you need a sound system to fully appreciate the site.

5. The Smugglers' Trail
www.southwest.uk.com/smuggling

This site tells an interesting story of the history of smuggling in the south west of England.
    Click on either the map or place names to explore the resorts. The adult will find the history interesting and the child will be excited with the tales, caves, haunts and locations. There are some wonderful place names, such as Dancing Ledge Cave, one of many smugglers' caves in the Isle of Purbeck, or Combe Cellars, a landing place on a remote part of the Teign.
    This would be a very useful site to help with creative writing, after visiting one of the resorts mentioned.

Section 4 Countryside

Websites

1. British Trees
www.british-trees.com

Everything you ever wanted to know about trees in Britain. The native tree guide link takes you to a list of trees in alphabetical order. Click on one and a detailed description, together with photographs, will be revealed. This is a very interesting and informative site.

2. A World Community of Old Trees
www.nyu.edu/projects/julian

This is a fascinating site containing links to a Tree Gallery, Tree Museum and Tree Talk. There is also an opportunity to add your own drawing or painting of trees. Clicking on 'Tree Gallery' will take you to trees from Venice and artists' trees. This is an American site with many links to other sites, which may need checking before being used with a class. Printing out some of the images may be sensible.

3. The Wonderful World of Trees
www.domtar.com/arbre/english/start.htm

A lovely colourful site, containing information, drawings, photographs and puzzles. There is also an alphabetically arranged list of trees in Northern America. Clicking on a map will reveal the types of trees growing in that area. This site is designed for both teachers and pupils to use. By clicking on the teacher's room icon at the bottom of the page, you will be able to access teaching sheets (very American in design). There is also a children's corner where you will find information, images and puzzles.

4. Featured Mysterious Sites of Britain
www.mysteriousbritain.co.uk

An excellent site which could accompany the section on the Countryside. There are many famous monuments featured on the site, for example, the Cerne Abbas Giant in Dorset, Stonehenge and Glamis Castle. There are links to other mysteries and legends.

5. White Horses of Britain
http://wiltshirewhitehorses.org.uk/others.html

This site lists many chalk white horses throughout Britain. There is a separate link for viewing photographs. Permission may be needed, however, to use one of the images.

6. The Long Man of Wilmington
www.sussexpast.co.uk/longman/longman.htm

This site is devoted to the historical and archaelogical evidence of the Long Man of Wilmington, on the South Downs. There are images, a detailed map and directions for getting to Wilmington. There is also a detailed further reading section.

General sites

1. Example of School Writing Trail
www.amherstschools.org.gg

Click on 'Literacy Trail' to view examples of children's work, produced while location writing in the school grounds. This was during a visit by Brian Moses.

2. Gnomes
www.foundus.com/jani/gnomes/welcome.html

Are you fascinated by the existence (or not) of gnomes? This site gives you a taste of the lives of gnomes – whether you believe or not! Gnomes live in the countryside. Farm Gnome for instance, resembles the house gnome but is of a more constant nature and is conservative in all matters. There are some delightful illustrations taken from the book *Gnomes*, by Wil Huygen and Rien Poortvliet.

8 Further Reading

Section 1 The School Environment

I Heard It In The Playground by Alan Ahlberg (Puffin), particularly the title poem.

Excuses, Excuses – Poems About School and *School's Out*, both edited by John Foster (OUP). Good sections on poems about playgrounds.

Why Do We Have To Go To School?, edited by John Foster (OUP).

It Takes One to Know One and *The Day Our Teacher Went Batty* – poetry by Gervase Phinn (Puffin).

Nine O'Clock Bell – Poems About School, chosen by Raymond Wilson (Puffin).

The School Year: Three Terms of Poems, chosen by Brian Moses (Macmillan).

School Poems, chosen by Jennifer Curry (Hippo Books, Scholastic).

The Playground Snake, by Brian Moses (Hopscotch, Franklin Watts).

Section 2 Castles, Houses and Ancient Monuments

The Boneyard Rap and Other Poems, by Wes Magee (Hodder Wayland). Poems about spooky activities in haunted places.

Spectacular Spooks, edited by Brian Moses (Macmillan).

The Old Stories, by Kevin Crossley-Holland (Dolphin). Retellings of old stories set in East Anglia and the Fen Country.

Scottish Poems, chosen by John Rice (Macmillan). Many poems about places in Scotland.

Around the World in Eighty Poems, selected by James Berry (Macmillan).

Section 3 The Seashore

The Mermaid's Purse, by Ted Hughes (Faber).

The Puffin Book of Salt-Sea Verse, compiled by Charles Causley (Puffin). Out of print but try libraries and secondhand bookshops.

The Forsaken Merman, edited by Berlie Doherty (Hodder Wayland).

Wild and Wonderful, wildlife poetry compiled by Tony Bradman (Hodder Wayland).

Seaside Poems, edited by Jill Bennett (OUP).

Section 4 Countryside

Season Songs, by Ted Hughes (Faber).

Earthways, Earthwise – Poems on Conservation, edited by Judith Nicholls (OUP).

A Year Full of Poems, edited by Michael Harrison and Christopher Stuart-Clark (OUP).

Green Poems, edited Jill Bennett (OUP).

A Puffin Year of Stories and Poems (Puffin).

The Works 2 – Poems on Every Subject and For Every Occasion, poems chosen by Brian Moses and Pie Corbett (Macmillan). Features a section on 'The environment'.

Section 5 Parks and Gardens

Green Days in Gardens – A Poetry Trail Through Ventnor Botanic Garden, produced by Lydia Fulleylove, Jacky Wilkinson and Paula Valledy (price £5). Excellent KS2 resource that can be adapted elsewhere. Details from Lydia Fulleylove, Literature Development Worker, Education Centre, Thompson House, Sandy Lane, Newport, Isle of Wight, PO30 3NA.

Books for Teaching Writing

Catapults and Kingfishers – Teaching Poetry in Primary Schools, by Brian Moses and Pie Corbett (OUP).

Drafting and Assessing Poetry – A Guide for Teachers, by Sue Dymoke (Paul Chapman Publishing).

The Poetry Book for Primary Schools, edited by Anthony Wilson with Sian Hughes (The Poetry Society).

Creating Writers, by James Carter (RoutledgeFalmer).

Writing Poetry – A Unique Structured Approach to Writing Poetry, books 1–4 by David Orme (Badger Publishing).

A Poetry Teacher's Toolkit, books 1–4 by Collette Drifte and Mike Jubb (David Fulton Publishers).

Just Imagine – Creative Ideas for Writing, by James Carter (David Fulton Publishers).

Read My Mind – Young Children, Poetry and Learning, by Fred Sedgwick (Routledge).